CALVERT VAUX, LANDSCAPE ARCHITECT

LALH

CALVERT VAUX
(1824–1895)

CALVERT VAUX, LANDSCAPE ARCHITECT

FRANCIS R. KOWSKY

LIBRARY OF AMERICAN LANDSCAPE HISTORY
AMHERST, MA

Library of American Landscape History
P.O. Box 1323
Amherst, MA 01004
www.lalh.org

Printed in China by Porter Print Group, LLC

Library of Congress Control Number: 2025942726
ISBN: 978-1-952620-42-3

Designed by Jonathan D. Lippincott
Set in Granjon

Distributed by
National Book Network
nbnbooks.com

Facing page 197: Ambrose Jackson, plate from *The Photographic Album* [Carte-de-visite Album of Central Park Views], 1860s, albumen silver print, gouache, varnish. Metropolitan Museum of Art.

Publication of this book was aided by a generous grant from Furthermore: a program of the J. M. Kaplan Fund

For Hélène. Every step in Central Park is a memory.

Woods, fields, mountains, and rivers *will* be more important than the houses that are built among them.

—Calvert Vaux, *Villas and Cottages* (1857)

Contents

Foreword

The well-deserved valorization of Frederick Law Olmsted—in which LALH has enthusiastically participated—is also clouding our understanding of the roots of the profession that Olmsted is often credited with having "fathered." Here Francis R. Kowsky offers a fresh look at the significant contributions of Calvert Vaux to the early park commissions undertaken with Olmsted, the work he accomplished on his own and in partnership with Samuel Parsons Jr., and the very origins of the field.

In addition to clarifying Vaux's important roles at Central Park, Prospect Park, and the Buffalo Parks system, Kowsky explores Vaux's designs of vest-pocket parks in Manhattan, large estates on the Hudson River (including Olana, where Vaux helped Frederic Church realize the Persian mansion and, surely, the landscape surrounding it), church grounds, campuses, and cemeteries. Through these projects, Kowsky traces an aesthetic forged in the Hudson River Valley, where Vaux began his all-too-brief American partnership with Andrew Jackson Downing.

Although Vaux's role in coaxing Olmsted to enter the profession via the Central Park competition is well known, Kowsky offers illuminating details. Knowing little about plants, having no drafting skills, and never having designed a landscape of that (or any) scale, Olmsted had to learn on the job, even as the park took shape under his tireless, often brilliant, administration. Despite this success, six years later, Vaux had to plead with a reluctant Olmsted to return from California to collaborate on a plan for Prospect Park. By the time Olmsted arrived, Vaux had moved forward independently, laying out much of the fundamental design on his own.

Kowsky also chronicles Vaux's auspicious christening of the new profession.

Encouraged by the example of his physician father and architects in England, Vaux was adamant that practitioners of landscape architecture—widely known at the time as landscape gardening—adopt a name that would convey professionalism to the public. At Vaux's insistence, "landscape architects," with its emphasis on design rather than horticulture, was signed on Central Park's Greensward plan. The term launched the Olmsted & Vaux partnership, and arguably the profession itself.

As a result of Vaux's influence, American landscape architects would soon follow the lead of architects in England who kept meticulous records and set fees based on the total cost of projects. Like their architectural brethren, landscape practitioners would also establish professional associations, publish periodicals featuring members' work, establish competitions, and join private clubs to socialize with fellow artists, politicians, and potential clients. By 1915 landscape architects would be represented, along with architects, at the American Academy in Rome.

It is not difficult to see how Vaux and his contributions to the nascent field have been marginalized. Olmsted was a persuasive writer, master strategist, savvy administrator, and political visionary. The charismatic force of his personality, his drive, and the success of his multigenerational office have tended to cast a wide beam. A gentle spirit with the soul of an artist, Calvert Vaux has been easy to overlook.

Robin Karson
Executive Director, LALH

Author's Preface

The nineteenth century was a transformative era for landscape architecture—a time when nature became an integral part of the social and cultural life of Europe and America. As urbanization spread rapidly across both continents, designing outdoor spaces evolved into a distinct and respected profession. In England, pioneers such as Humphry Repton, Joseph Paxton, and John Claudius Loudon led the way, their work paralleled by influential figures on the European continent, including Prince Hermann von Pückler-Muskau in Germany and Édouard André and Jean-Charles Adolphe Alphand in France. These visionaries laid the foundation for modern urban parks, public gardens, and private estates.

In the United States, three names from this era stand out: Andrew Jackson Downing, Frederick Law Olmsted, and Calvert Vaux. While substantial scholarship has explored the philosophies and aesthetic principles of Downing and Olmsted, little attention has been accorded to their colleague. With this book I have turned the focus to Vaux, examining the enduring legacy of artistry, humanity, and practicality that defined his landscape work.

In my earlier book, *Country, Park, and City: The Architecture and Life of Calvert Vaux,* I aimed to paint a comprehensive portrait of this remarkable individual, who arrived in New York in 1850 from his native England bringing with him a deep understanding of architecture, an appreciation for natural scenery, and a rare sensitivity to the potential of public parks. These were uncommon qualities at the time. Vaux's life and work in America over the latter half of the nineteenth century encompassed a wide range of achievements, challenges, and historical contexts. My earlier study laid the foundation for the present book.

Over the years since that first publication, I have come to realize that Vaux's career as a landscape architect deserves a more focused and dedicated examination—distinct from his significant contributions as an architect. This book revisits his passion for nature and his belief in the vital role that natural landscapes play in the health and well-being of urban life. It also recognizes his efforts to establish landscape architecture as a respected and lasting profession. Vaux felt a duty to guide future generations, offering a vision of what landscape design could be in a rapidly changing world.

By highlighting his major landscape projects, I have sought not merely to recount events but to explore the range, depth, and beauty of Vaux's work. New research and fresh perspectives have allowed me to see his legacy in a new light. I hope readers will come to appreciate the subtlety and complexity with which he adapted the natural world to serve human needs and enrich human experience. Whether you are encountering Calvert Vaux for the first time or returning to his story after reading my earlier biography, I invite you to join me in exploring this essential chapter of his life—and of the evolving American landscape he helped shape.

CALVERT VAUX, LANDSCAPE ARCHITECT

Rustic bridge over the Gill, Central Park. Photo by Sara Cedar Miller, courtesy Central Park Conservancy.

Overview

"Absolutely the most ingenious, industrious and indefatigable man in his profession"

Calvert Vaux's contributions to the modern practice of landscape architecture are not well known, yet they can scarcely be overstated. Active as both architect and landscape architect, Vaux demonstrated remarkable sensitivity to the way buildings should relate to their surroundings and the way landscapes should be laid out to best meet the requirements of their users. He exercised a gifted ability to grasp a design problem and to produce a clear-minded and elegant solution that addressed both practical and aesthetic imperatives. He was, to Frederick Law Olmsted, whose reputation far exceeds that of his friend and collaborator, "absolutely the most ingenious, industrious and indefatigable man in his profession of all that I have known for the study of plans to meet complicated requirements."[1]

In 1850, at the age of twenty-five, the young aspiring London architect had the good fortune of being invited to collaborate with the celebrated landscape gardener and architectural writer Andrew Jackson Downing (1815–1852). Known to history as the "Apostle of Taste" and the "Prophet with Honor," in his own day Downing was frequently described as the "American Loudon"—a reference to the Scottish botanist Claudius Loudon (1783–1843), who had risen to prominence in the early nineteenth century as a horticulturist and landscape gardener. Both Downing and Loudon had gained a wide reputation in the English-speaking world through the publication of many articles and books intended for both upper- and middle-class audiences. These writings promoted the gardenesque style of landscape design, the gothic style for the architecture of rural residences, and the desirability of parks in growing cities. Vaux would have been familiar with these works.

In America, Vaux soon came to appreciate the veneration of nature and domesticity that informed Downing's theories and designs for houses and grounds, sharing "with Downing the labor of preaching for the first time in this country the gospel of taste and beauty in connection with country houses and estates," as one contemporary noted.[2] In his partnership with Olmsted, Vaux played a major role in launching the American urban park movement and establishing landscape architecture as a profession.

Under the firm name Olmsted, Vaux & Co., the two men turned first to Central Park in 1857, then to Prospect Park in 1865, followed by the innovative park and parkway system designed for Buffalo beginning in 1868. Many other municipalities hired the partners to make plans for parks in their communities. Olmsted and Vaux's recommendations are summarized in reports that propose comprehensive schemes to incorporate parks and boulevards into the cityscape based on cogent assessments of urban conditions, a reflection of their keen eye for capitalizing on local natural features and scenery. Among these collaborations were City Park in Philadelphia (1867), Washington Park (present Fort Greene Park) in Brooklyn (1867), a park at Newark, New Jersey (1867), Walnut Hill Park, New Britain, Connecticut (1870), South Park in Fall River, Massachusetts (1868), and South Park in Chicago (1871). Riverside, Illinois (1868), a planned community outside Chicago, represented a private venture that raised the ideal of parklike suburban home life to a new level of significance. The verdant grounds of Gallaudet College in Washington, DC (1860s; where their associate Frederick Clarke Withers designed the buildings), opened a new chapter in campus planning.

Among the partners' many patrons in the 1860s and early 1870s were the boards of enlightened psychiatric institutions. The Bloomingdale Asylum in New York City (on the present site of Columbia University), the Hartford Retreat (today the Institute of Living) in Hartford, Connecticut, and state mental hospitals at Poughkeepsie and Buffalo required their services. Their plans represented the modification of their park design principles for landscapes of healing. "In this approach," writes the landscape historian Jennifer Thomas, "farm, outdoor recreation, pleasure grounds, and exposure to rural landscape views were considered fundamental to patient therapy."[3] Vaux himself was a brief resident at Dr. D. Tilden Brown's Bloomingdale Asylum in the early 1860s. When Olmsted visited him there, he found his friend hallucinating and talking "incessantly of glass, colors, and drapery."[4] The delirium passed quickly, and within days Vaux was back working hard—a probable cause of his breakdown, along with a bout of typhoid fever.

Mental instability seems not to have darkened his life again, but personal experience surely disposed Calvert Vaux to devote his skills with sympathy to the care of the mentally ill. On the rebound, he became architect of the Sheppard Asylum near Baltimore (the present Sheppard and Enoch Pratt Hospital), which he designed in Olmsted's absence during the war years. At the heart of the philosophy that both he and Olmsted—who would live his last five years at McLean Asylum—subscribed to were Downing's earlier words on the curative power of nature. "Many a fine intellect, overtasked and wrecked in the too ardent pursuit of wealth or power," Vaux's first partner had observed, "is fondly courted back to reason, and more quiet joys, by the dusky, cool walks of the asylum, where peace and rural beauty do not refuse to dwell."[5]

On his own, Vaux also planned smaller parks and private landscapes. For many years after parting from Olmsted, he served as landscape architect to the New York City Department of Public Parks, and in that capacity, continued to add to the Central Park landscape and to design parks and squares for New York at a time when the metropolis was rapidly evolving into adulthood. In his later years, Vaux designed small tranquil greenspaces, "vest-pocket parks," in the despairingly crowded tenement districts of Lower Manhattan.

Vaux was also engaged by a number of private clients. The shipping magnate William R. Grace hired him for his Long Island estate, Gracefield; Samuel Tilden, the unsuccessful presidential contender, had him lay out Greystone, his property in Yonkers, New York; the pharmaceutical entrepreneur Alexander Hudnut commissioned Vaux to create the grounds around his residence in Llewellyn Park, New Jersey; and John Horner Wisner, a wealthy merchant in the China trade, called on Vaux for The Clearing, his suburban residence in Summit, New Jersey. The house and seven-acre grounds that Vaux designed in Oxford, Mississippi, for the plantation owner and founder of the University of Mississippi Thomas E. B. Pegues, was the most geographically far-flung of such commissions. (William Faulkner portrayed Pegues's homestead, later named Ammadelle, as Horace Benbow's house in his 1929 novel *Sartoris*.)[6] For middle-class families eager to escape the city for green suburbs, Vaux gave valuable advice on laying out grounds around their homes in various publications.

Downing was a proponent of the rural cemetery movement, a new stylistic episode in landscape architecture that Vaux would likewise advance. Vaux's 1860 design for Hillside Cemetery in Middletown, New York, was followed by others on this model. For the trustees of Trinity Cemetery (1881) in Upper Manhattan, Vaux produced a plan that Olmsted admired greatly, even advising others to learn from it. Vaux's plan for Riverside Cemetery (1887) in Macon, Georgia—which the *Atlanta Constitution* noted "was being made into one of the most beautiful burial grounds in the south"—transformed the remains of a Confederate installation on the Ocmulgee River into a place of reverential contemplation. In a similar way, at Riverview Cemetery (1888) in Trenton, New Jersey, Vaux capitalized on the evocative scenery along the shore of the Delaware.

Vaux also excelled at the design of park structures, an emerging category of architecture in America that included summer houses, bridges, boat houses, boat landings, seats, and other incidental constructions. These adjuncts to the visitor's park experience were meant to provide shelter, facilitate movement, invite lingering, and encourage socializing. And, the art historian Kerry Dean Carso has noted, these "playful, whimsical structures" were intended to impart a carefree spirit to the landscape.[7] Vaux made park architecture a specialty and was the first practitioner in the United States to contribute significantly to this realm of design. Some of America's most beautiful nineteenth-century bridges are those that Vaux created in Central Park, where he elevated the overpass to high art. In other instances, he based his fanciful creations on vernacular rural tradition, much as a classical composer might seek inspiration from folk melodies. Buffalo's resplendent Parade House, a lavish setting for egalitarian amusement where visitors might come to eat, drink, dance, or watch a play, the Dairy in Central Park, and the Concert Grove Pavilion in Prospect Park exemplify the range of his artistry.

Whatever form his park structures took, they conformed to Vaux's rule of thumb that they be "subordinated" to the landscape that embraced them. To this end, locations were carefully chosen, materials and color aptly selected, and leading lines of the design adjusted to the features of the terrain. An early example is the Stone Arch in the Ramble, one of the first structures completed in Central Park. Carrying a path over a ravine, the rustic, vine-clad archway of weather-beaten stone nestles discreetly between two giant boulders native to the site. Another fine example is Vaux's exotic Spire Head House gazebo, which formerly stood in Buffalo's Delaware Park. The structure settled so neatly into a surrounding of trees and shrubs that it was barely visible from the lake it overlooked. The First Sister Island bridge on the Niagara Reservation, designed by Vaux in 1893, still carries visitors across a rocky woodland rivulet on a low arch constructed of water-worn local stone. "Nature, first and 2nd and 3rd—Architecture after a while," Vaux declared his guiding design principle for Bethesda Terrace in Central Park. It might have been his universal mantra where park structures were concerned.[8]

Several photographic portraits of Calvert Vaux as well as pictures of him in Central Park confirm the physical description that appeared in newspapers at the time of his death. Of medium build, measuring four feet, ten inches tall, Vaux was short even by the standards of his day. From other sources, we know that gray hair and a beard set off a ruddy complexion. He wore gold-rimmed glasses for his myopia and often sported a black derby hat. And he had a fondness for bow ties, shared by later generations of architects.[9]

Vaux's contemporaries referred to him as often distracted, wrestling with some inner conundrum, while seemingly oblivious to his surroundings. It is not surprising to learn that he exuded an endearing absent-mindedness. Yet, his contemporaries also regarded him as a man of sociable disposition and convivial nature. A regular at the Century Association, Vaux enjoyed flavorsome food and wine and the company of creative and interesting companions. More so than his good friend "Fred" Olmsted, Vaux displayed an affable sense of humor. Under stress, Vaux could also be flustered and irascible. His brother-in-law Jervis McEntee, who was probably his closest friend, lamented that "Cal" could nurse a grievance for far too long. Olmsted's wife Mary likewise found him prone to annoying persistent behavior, as when she complained of his "chivying English disposition."[10] Being publicly ignored as the co-creator of Central Park was an abiding source of resentment.

Calvert Vaux's eventful career began in his native England. He was born in London in 1824, the son of a respected surgeon. He grew up on historic Pudding Lane, not far from Sir Christopher Wren's giant column commemorating the Great Fire of London of 1666, which had started there. Vaux received a traditional education at the venerable Merchant Taylors' School, founded in the sixteenth century. Later he studied architecture under the tutelage of Lewis Nockalls Cottingham, a well-known practitioner of the Gothic Revival who was especially in demand for the restoration of medieval churches. Cottingham also designed large country dwellings, such as castellated Snelston Hall in Derbyshire, where he laid out the grounds in a parklike setting of winding paths and informal plantings. In his own house, Cottingham possessed an extensive library. Here young Vaux could have consulted works by Humphry Repton, John Claudius Loudon, William Sawrey Gilpin, Uvedale Price, and other British and French eighteenth- and early nineteenth-century authors of books on natural scenery and landscape gardening.

The roots of Vaux's fertile imagination as a landscape architect and park designer lay here and in the English countryside. "England . . . is eminently the land of the picturesque," wrote Isaac Taylor, a poet and author Vaux admired. "Although what is grand or romantic is confined to a few districts," Taylor observed, "what is deliciously beautiful, and that which invites the pencil, and feeds the taste, presents itself in every county. Few countries, if any in the world, are so thickly set with points of view, such as the landscape painter stops to notice; and those who would establish themselves in the rural mode, with a view to the health and enjoyments of a family, may take their course in almost any direction, and find spots where nothing which external circumstances can supply will be wanting to secure the sweet felicity of a domestic country life."[11] In 1846, Vaux embarked upon an extended tour of Britain and the Continent with his young friend the architect George Truefitt. Theirs was a formative journey that redrew the boundaries of Vaux's tyro knowledge and creative imagination.

In the summer of 1850, at the invitation of Andrew Jackson Downing, Vaux, who was struggling to find a foothold in the British architectural profession, emigrated to America. The two men had met at an Architectural Association exhibition in London where Vaux had drawings on display. While on his first European tour, Downing had gone to the Association, which enrolled mostly younger practitioners, in search of an architect to work with him at his home, Highland Gardens, in Newburgh, New York. Through his widely read books and articles, Downing commanded something of a revolution in the way well-to-do and middle-class American homeowners, whose numbers were ever increasing, thought about their houses and gardens. "Before his day," remarked the popular chronicler Edgar Mayhew Bacon, ". . . in the laying out of rural estates, grotesque and chaotic arrangement of natural material was the rule rather than the exception. Mr. Downing not only possessed taste and sense, but he managed to impart them to others."[12] Downing also maintained a prosperous nursery business which he and his older brother Charles, an authority on pomology, had inherited from their father. Andrew had gained a national reputation as an expert on fruit culture with the 1845 publication of his often-reprinted book *The Fruits and Fruit Trees of America*. Other books and articles on architecture soon issued from his pen.

Encouraged by his literary successes, Downing, who was seven years Vaux's senior, hoped to capitalize on his reputation by greatly expanding the number of clients who came to him for designs for houses and the grounds around them. "He had two qualities that are not always combined in one individual," observed

Bacon, "namely, artistic sensibility and practical sense. The latter enabled him to make the former effective."[13] To achieve his ambition, Downing needed the services of a professional architect. He found the perfect match in Vaux, who in addition to his architectural capability possessed a sensitive eye for landscape and the appeal of natural scenery.

When Vaux arrived at Downing's home, he entered a world that was distinctly different from the one he had known in London. During the slow steamer ride northward from New York to Newburgh (it took several hours), his imagination had time to accommodate itself to his new surroundings. As his boat approached the harbor, Vaux would have seen unfold before him the mountain-framed view of Newburgh Bay. "From the shore below, we have gained one of the most perfect views of this noble port of the Hudson's course," wrote Vaux's soon-to-be friend the poet William Cullen Bryant. "We see the entrance of the Highlands, and the broad expanse of water lying between this and the town . . . put one in the mood for the first sight of the grand aspects of mountain and stream upon which he is to look."[14]

Others shared Bryant's enthusiasm. Since the early years of the century, artists such as Thomas Doughty, Thomas Cole, and Asher B. Durand had celebrated the romantic beauty of the Hudson River Valley. "The Hudson for natural magnificence is unsurpassed," wrote Cole, who attached spiritual significance to the region, in his 1836 "Essay on American Scenery." Turning a blind eye to the displacement of Indigenous peoples, slavery, and the violence of the Anti-Rent War around them, popular writers such as Bryant and Nathaniel Parker Willis extolled the region's natural treasures. By midcentury, the Hudson Valley and Catskills had become a refuge for many seeking respite from the hustle and ugliness of the city. Steamboat and rail lines made travel comparatively easy for people of means, who frequented hotels like the scenic Catskill Mountain House, Laurel House, and Mohonk Mountain House. "Over the course of the nineteenth century," observed the historian David Schuyler, " . . . there emerged a growing recognition that the valley was more than farmsteads and local communities—that it was a place of transcendent importance to a regional and national cultural identity."[15] The "sanctified landscape" of the Hudson River Valley would have a lasting influence on Vaux's creative imagination and would figure prominently in his personal life.

Stepping through the gate into Highland Gardens, Vaux came face-to-face with one of America's beloved designed landscapes. Modest by British standards, Downing's charming Tudor-style house nestled in five acres of lush grounds. His home environment signified the ideal of American domestic life well lived in a leisurely world of hearth and verdure. Trees and understory plantings framed the dwelling and screened the workaday world of the nursery business from view, winding garden paths led to embowered rustic seats, and a broad lawn opened the area in front of the house to a view of the river. Downing's elevated property, indeed, possessed surpassing vistas of the Hudson Highlands. Vaux himself recorded the beauties of the place in drawings, two of which survive as woodcuts published in *The Horticulturist,* the national magazine of "rural art and rural taste" that Downing edited.

Advanced taste in style paired with a vital intellectual atmosphere. Soon after his arrival in America, Vaux manifested the reformist spirit and liberal values that were in the air at Highland Gardens. His espousal of social democracy may well have begun with lively discussions on the differences between social conditions in England and America which took place when the Swedish feminist Frederika Bremer visited Downing. Vaux's polemical essay "Should a Republic Encourage the Arts," which appeared in *The Horticulturist* in 1852, would serve as his enduring statement on the subject. A few years afterward, he affirmed in print that "public baths, gymnasiums, theatres, music-halls, libraries, lecture-rooms, parks, gardens, picture-galleries, museums, schools, and everything that is needed for the liberal education of an intelligent freeman's children, can easily be obtained by the genuine republican if he will only take the trouble to *want* them."[16] He later told

Vaux, "View from the Lawn," *Horticulturist* (January 1853).

Henry Gritten, *Springside: Center Circle*, 1852. Frances Lehman Loeb Art Center, Vassar College.

Olmsted, who became publicly identified with progressive political causes, that he was "quite as much a lover of the People as you or any man can be. I show it in my way, You in Yours."[17]

Downing's office soon attracted clients possessed of ample resources to spend on their home and grounds. Business was conducted at first in an unused bedroom. Soon, however, Downing was able to erect a small office wing. There, Downing and Vaux were assisted by Frederick Clarke Withers, another British-trained architect who arrived in 1851, and other helpers, including the future art critic and chronicler of Central Park, Clarence Cook. One of the first persons to patronize the convivial enterprise was Matthew Vassar, the Poughkeepsie brewer-turned-educational-philanthropist. Vassar anticipated erecting a grand new residence that Vaux worked up in a series of drawings that bore the stamp of the newly arrived professional. In addition, Downing and Vaux transformed Vassar's twenty-seven-acre property into a marvel of informal landscape design. The tranquil country retreat at the edge of town provided its wealthy owner with over two miles of meandering walks and drives. Vaux described Springside, the name Vassar bestowed on his personal domain, as "being full of easy sweeps and gentle undulations, . . . somewhat secluded and park-like in character."[18]

Another early client was Warren Delano, a successful importer of goods from the Far East who resided nearby. He engaged the pair to remodel his existing home, Algonac, into a modern Italianate villa. In laying out the property around the house, Vaux would have learned from Downing how to plant for all-season enjoyment: spruce and hemlock for winter color; oak, beech, maple, and some exotic species from China for other times of the year. For Daniel Parish, who had accumulated a vast fortune from a booming dry goods business in New York, Downing and Vaux created an imposing summer residence at Newport. The Palladian-style seaside villa that Vaux designed (today open as a public museum, Beechwood Mansion) overlooked lawns that extended down to the shore. The borrowed view conjured a sublime sense of distance. Appropriating natural scenery at hand would play a part in public parks that Vaux later designed with Olmsted. On the land side, a large, comfortable veranda wedded the dwelling to a tranquil garden.

Undoubtedly, the most sympathetic client Vaux got to know as Downing's partner was Henry Winthrop Sargent. The banker son of the Boston painter Henry Sargent, he was a friend of Downing's who took an avid interest in horticulture. In later years, he would edit a posthumous edition of Downing's *Treatise on the Theory and Practice of Landscape Gardening.* Between 1847 and 1849, Sargent had traveled extensively in England "mainly to see all the country places worth seeing, large or small."[19] From that experience evolved his desire to enlarge his already ample residence overlooking the Hudson River at Fishkill Landing (now Beacon, New York).

Vaux took charge of remodeling Sargent's Wodenethe (Welsh for "wooded hill"), transforming the sedate Federal-style manse into a spreading villa that featured carefully planned prospects of spacious lawns and Newburgh Bay. Each window, Sargent was pleased to report, held "one distinct and separate view . . . making, as it were, a series of cabinet pictures."[20] From the library a riparian panorama opened, with two distinct landscapes on either side of a stand of trees: one surveyed a wooded point across the river, the other featured a quiet island with Storm King Mountain in the background. From the breakfast room a visitor could contemplate a river prospect toward Newburgh. And on the front or entrance side of the villa, away from the river, residents looked out on a spacious parklike scene of lawn shaded by native oaks growing singly or in groups.[21]

The most important commission of Vaux's time with Downing came in 1851 when President Millard Fillmore, an upstate New Yorker with an appreciation of horticulture, succeeded in lobbying Congress to hire Downing to lay out an

Wodenethe, 1886. Courtesy Arnold Arboretum.

"View from the Library Window, at Wodenethe, looking South." From Downing, *Treatise*.

extensive park in Washington. The enterprise involved nothing less, said Vaux, than "a comprehensive plan for landscape gardening that included the Smithsonian grounds, and also the whole of the public park proposed to connect the President's house [White House] with the Capitol."[22] No one in America had yet conceived of a single designed landscape on such a scale. It was the first major publicly funded project of its kind in the nation's history, intended to raise the image of the city in the eyes of the nation and the world. Moreover, Fillmore's ambitious plans for Washington may have marked an early instance of the use of landscape for political ends. The year before, Fillmore had signed the Compromise of 1850, a controversial piece of legislation that, despite its serious flaws, he and others hoped would preserve Northern and Southern solidarity. Downing and Vaux's elaborate upgrade of the governmental core of Washington showcased the capital's centrality in national life at a time when federal unity was under grave threat.

The historic undertaking provided Vaux unprecedented experience in the challenges of planning and constructing extensive grounds for public use and enjoyment. Vaux might well have been at his side in Newburgh when Downing wrote his

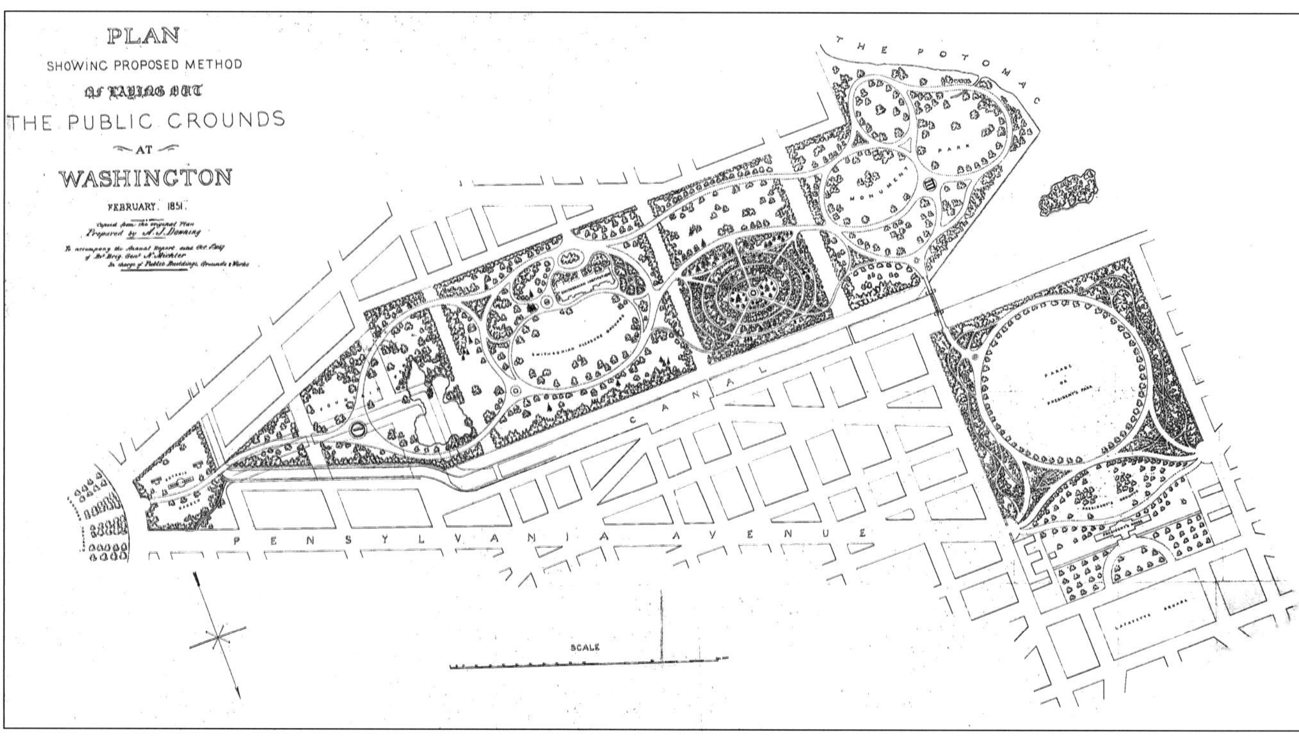

Downing, *Plan Showing Proposed Method of Laying Out the Public Grounds at Washington, February 1851.* National Archives / A. J. Downing.

B. F. Smith, *Washington, D.C. with projected improvements*, 1852, color lithograph. Library of Congress Prints and Photographs Division.

description of the plans for "The Public Grounds at Washington." The many acres were to be treated in such a manner that they

> would undoubtedly become a Public School of Instruction in everything that relates to the tasteful arrangement of parks and grounds, and the growth and culture of trees, while they would serve, more than anything else that could be devised, to embellish and give interest to the Capital. The straight lines and broad Avenues of the streets of Washington would be pleasantly relieved and contrasted by the beauty of curved lines and natural groups of trees in the various parks.

Downing's intention was threefold:

> 1st: To form a national Park, which should be an ornament to the Capital of the United States; 2nd: To give an example of the natural style of Landscape Gardening which may have an influence on the general taste of the Coun-

try; 3rd: To form a collection of all the trees that will grow in the climate of Washington, and, by having these trees plainly labelled with their popular and scientific names, to form a public museum of living trees and shrubs.[23]

Reading such statements today reminds us of the nascent state of landscape architecture at the time. Downing did not even use the term; rather he referred to his occupation as "landscape gardening." Perhaps with Downing in mind, a few years later, Ralph Waldo Emerson listed "the landscape gardener" as one of "the new professions."[24]

Vaux's time with Downing came to an abrupt end in July 1852 when a catastrophic explosion occurred on the steamboat bound for New York on which Downing, his wife Mary, and her family were traveling. Downing, a strong swimmer, helped save many, but eventually a panicked passenger dragged him under. When the dead were pulled ashore, Downing was among them. Arriving at Yonkers where the accident had occurred, Vaux had the grim task of identifying his body. With Downing's death and Fillmore's departure from the presidency in March 1853, the capital work, which would have included a triumphal arch that Vaux had sketched, languished. The grand national endeavor was never completed as planned. In 1856, however, Vaux succeeded in having a large Carrara marble urn of his design placed near the Smithsonian Institution to honor his friend and mentor's memory.[25]

Working with Downing as both a designer of buildings and a collaborator on the layout of grounds, Vaux had gained a valuable foothold in his adopted country in the budding professions of architecture and landscape design. When he moved from Highland Gardens soon after Downing's death, he took with him the knowledge of how to conduct a professional architecture and landscape design practice. He had learned valuable lessons in how to meet the demands of diverse commissions and to deal with influential clients. Perhaps not well known enough to be considered heir to Downing's elevated reputation, Vaux, nevertheless, had secured a place in influential circles of well-informed New York society. For the next four years, Vaux stayed on in Newburgh. As Downing's professional successor, he continued to attract commissions for dwellings of many sorts. Nor did the personal memories of his departed friend and mentor dim. When his second child was born in 1856, he named him after the man to whom he owed so much. Downing Vaux (d. 1926), like his father and his namesake, would devote himself to landscape architecture, both as a practitioner and as a promoter of its professionalization.

Vaux, "Design No. 6, Perspective View." From *Villas and Cottages* (1857).

The following year, Vaux published the book he had been preparing for some time, *Villas and Cottages.* The handsome portfolio of attractive houses, ranging from small to large, was addressed to the general home-building public more than to fellow architects or builders. Describing residences he had designed during his time in Newburgh, Vaux showed that he had been sought out by middle- and working-class clients in addition to people of wealth. For good reason, Vaux included houses that had been designed during his halcyon days at Highland Gardens. Proudly noting the late prestigious partnership on the title page, Vaux linked his name with that of the revered Downing in the minds of his readers. His book enjoyed a long shelf life. Harper & Brothers issued later editions in 1864 (revised with additional material, including representations of Central Park), 1867, 1872, and 1874. These kept the memory of the Vaux–Downing association alive in the public's imagination.

In the year of Downing's birth, Vaux, Mary, and their two young sons (Calvert Bowyer, born in 1855) relocated to New York.[26] Since Vaux's arrival in America, he had attached himself to the busy life of the thriving metropolis. He was well aware that for over a decade, civic leaders there had been talking about the need to establish a large public park for its citizens. The call was urgent before all the land on Manhattan Island was occupied by buildings. Downing himself had lent his voice and influence to the cause. In 1853 state officials approved funds to purchase seven hundred acres of land in the center of Manhattan for recreational use. A board of commissioners assumed authority to oversee development of the ambitious project. They hired the military engineer Egbert Viele to map the largely unoccupied land and to devise a plan for what became known as Central Park.[27] Dismayed at Viele's uninspired scheme, Vaux, now a city resident, leveraged his reputation as Downing's former partner to persuade the commissioners reconsider. He advocated for opening the park design to a competition.

Once the contest was announced in the fall of 1857, Vaux contacted Frederick Law Olmsted, whom he knew chiefly by reputation as author of the book *Walks and Talks of an American Farmer in England,* to propose they collaborate on an entry. At the time, Olmsted had charge of the considerable labor force the city had assembled to prepare the ground for construction of the new park. Prior to that, in 1856, Olmsted had spent six months in London, where he devoted much of his time to looking closely at the city's parks. His interest in public landscapes, he said, was "not at all from the official point of view or a gardener's point of view, but from that of a citizen seeking rest, refreshment, recreation in them." Yet, Olmsted, who was familiar with the writings on landscape by Repton and others, also had a keen eye for nature and "the gardener's point of view." By the time of the Central Park competition, he proclaimed that he had acquired "a better understanding of what they [parks] should be than any other man of American birth and breeding."[28] According to Vaux's protégé Samuel Parsons Jr., Vaux, the English-trained professional, soon came to have "profound respect for Mr. Olmsted's constructive imagination and artistic power."[29] In Olmsted, Vaux found someone who matched his own powers of observation, habit of mind, and love of nature. With the Central Park competition, Olmsted found his way into Vaux's life.

"Coming into business at 40 with the spirit of a boy of 20, allowances had to be made by an old hand like me," Vaux later good-humoredly told Olmsted (who was actually thirty-five, only two years Vaux's junior, when they created the Greensward plan). Whatever he thought of Olmsted's inexperience, Vaux recognized his brilliance and was prescient of his future. "I also knew that you . . . would outrank me if you also threw all you had into the scale and I tempted you in every way to do it—caring not a damn about the outranking but desiring an agreeable employment and to help supply a public need."[30] "Both physically and philosophically," wrote the architectural historian George Tatum, "Vaux provided the link between Downing, the first American-born landscape gardener to achieve an international reputation, and Olmsted, whose name has become virtually synonymous with American park design."[31] Their joining forces was a momentous event for the progress of American urbanism and the rise of the profession of landscape architecture. Only Vaux's death in 1895 would end the friendship that began in that winter of 1857–58.

Another person who figured significantly in Vaux's career as a result of Central Park was the attorney and reform political operative Andrew Haswell Green (1820–1903). Known to history as the "Father of Greater New York," Green was an indefatigable promoter of improvements to the civic life of his adopted city (he came to New York from Worcester, Massachusetts). These included the creation of the American Museum of Natural History and the New York Public Library, and the preservation of Joseph-François Mangin and John McComb Jr.'s 1803 City Hall. His farsighted North River Bridge proposal would have spanned the Hudson long before the George Washington Bridge was built. Green also took an active role in the campaign to have New York State acquire the land around Niagara Falls for a park.

Vaux became Green's close associate on many endeavors. These included a trip to London in 1868 to inspect the new Underground with an eye to creating a similar system in New York. Vaux wrote a lengthy report on the subject that must surely be one of the earliest documents in the history of subway transit in America. At Green's invitation, he also served on the boards of the Metropolitan Museum of Art, the American Scenic and Historic Preservation Society, the Commission of Municipal Consolidation Inquiry, and the Greater New-York Commission. Reflecting on Vaux's membership on the two commissions that sought to join the separate boroughs into a single entity, Green acknowledged that no one had been more effective than Vaux in the "adornment of the municipalities whose union is the purpose of our meeting."[32]

Vaux and Green first came to know each other in the early days of the Central Park project, when Green served as city comptroller. In that capacity, he played the role of financial watchdog, monitoring all expenditures for the park's construction. Almost from the start, however, personal animosity grew between Green, a stickler for procedure and accountability, and Olmsted, who, as superintendent, felt that he should have a free hand in carrying out the work of building the park. Olmsted soon found that his position involved sparring with a tightfisted, distrustful functionary. The bad feelings would last throughout the lifetimes of both men, although Green respected Olmsted's talents as a landscape architect.

Among good government people, Green enjoyed a high reputation for honesty and integrity. The diarist George Templeton Strong noted that "the only person I ever heard speak ill of him was F. L. Olmsted," and was quick to add that "Olmsted has a rather *mauvaise langue*."[33] Green was "a Puritan from New England and with the virtues and faults of the race," remarked Parsons, whom Green knew well, "but he won his way and carried his points with great pertinacity and success. I doubt if Central Park, as we know it, would ever have been built, except for Mr. Green's ability to coax or force appropriations from Albany, and, above all, for his superb loyalty to the artists and scientists employed by the Park Department."[34]

The construction of Central Park, which began in 1858, marked the true beginning of the public park movement in America and the genesis of a partnership that would place Vaux and Olmsted at the forefront of that movement. Yet the trajectory of their reputation faltered when Olmsted went off to Washington in 1861 to serve the Union war effort as executive secretary of the United States Sanitary Commission, a nongovernmental organization dedicated to providing medical assistance to Union troops. Then, in 1863, he relinquished his post and moved with his family to California. Olmsted went there, like so many others, seeking his fortune in gold mining.

During these years when their paths in life diverged widely, Vaux did his utmost to bring his friend back to New York. In a series of ardent letters, Vaux repeatedly summoned Olmsted to return to what Vaux saw as his true calling. Declaring that God had meant Olmsted to see his destiny in "our art," Vaux asserted that "although he may have something different for you to do yet he cannot have anything nobler in store for you."[35] In fact, Vaux regarded Olmsted's decision to leave Central Park as more than a grievous personal mistake; he also saw it as a betrayal of the nascent discipline of landscape architecture. Olmsted owed it to this new profession he represented to resume his former post. "You have allowed yourself to stand before the Public as Architect in Chief of the Central Park," Vaux declared, "and it is useless to argue that no responsibility attaches to you."[36] In his opinion, Olmsted had placed the future of that profession in jeopardy:

> The Gold mine people and the oil people get rich—most of the artists remain poor, except they prostitute their abilities. In a properly civilised republic this should not be, in our republic it need not be if representative men were only true to their (implied) oaths of office. The designers of Parks if successful in one way should be successful in the other. In the present state of art development in the country, it is very necessary indeed for those who have the power to exert themselves to protect the strictly legitimate pecuniary interests con-

nected with the pursuits they follow for each in its turn must be proved to be profitable or young men of ability will be deterred from venturing into it.[37]

Vaux held that he and Olmsted had an obligation to the future of their profession to see that Central Park succeeded according to their plans. It would be, he asserted, "a burning shame and a reprehensible mistake on our part if the Central Park slips up as a confused jumble of which there is nothing quotable as precedent, that will help our successors."[38] It was, he later wrote, the means of elevating landscape architecture, "an unaccredited but important pursuit," to a place among "the best interests of humanity."[39]

In Vaux's view, their work at Central Park had laid the foundations for a new discipline, which he insisted, over Olmsted's initial objection, on calling "landscape architecture." Olmsted in the beginning saw their challenges more in terms of management and administration rather than invention and design. Vaux argued that, like the creators of buildings, they were foremost artists and that "it is the art title we want to set out ahead, and may it command its position [above] administration, management, funds, commission, popularity and everything else. . . . As administration with art attached as makeweight, the thing is in the wrong shape." He even chided Olmsted for his workaholic preoccupation with organization, being dismayed to find him at Central Park with his "porcupine arrangement of Foremen's reports 70 to each pocket and one in your mouth so that you never had a word to say to a friend."[40] To Vaux, landscape architecture was a newborn sister to the traditional fine arts. "In the arts of architecture, painting and sculpture," he reflected years later, "the results are determined by the limitations of the human brain and hand, but in the art of landscape design no such boundary line is recognizable."[41]

While Olmsted was off directing mining operations in California, Vaux was engaged in discussions with the City of Brooklyn to design a vast new park there. By the summer of 1865, he had determined boundaries and the general outline of the Prospect Park plan. He hoped that the potential of a new park job with a different group of commissioners from those who had aggravated them in Manhattan would entice Olmsted to come back from California. When Vaux also secured the partners' return to official positions at Central Park, Olmsted finally relented. Whether Olmsted realized it or not, he had now fixed upon the career that would set his name forever in the annals of American culture. Olmsted himself later admitted that had it not been for Vaux, "I should not have been a landscape architect, I should have been a farmer."[42]

Their revived partnership endured until 1872. By then, Olmsted explained, there were "matters between us in which each thought the other wrong-headed."[43] For his part, Vaux had in hand at the time three large architectural commissions that he surely believed would demand his fullest attention: the Metropolitan Museum of Art, the American Museum of Natural History, and a vast pavilion to house the Centennial Exhibition in Philadelphia. In 1883, Olmsted left New York for the quiet suburb of Brookline, Massachusetts, where, in the manner of Downing, he established his home and office, to which he gave the idyllic name Fairsted.

Vaux chose to remain in New York. From 1881 until his death, he served, with some exceptions, as landscape architect to the Department of Public Parks. In this capacity he eventually came to oversee numerous parks and greenspaces throughout the city. By the time of his death, Vaux had design responsibility for the landscapes of Central, Riverside, Morningside, Van Cortlandt, and Bronx Parks, and the New York Botanical Garden, as well as many smaller parks, including Mount Morris, East River, Bryant, Union Square, and Battery Parks.[44] City squares—among them Washington Square and City Hall Park—also fell under his jurisdiction, in addition to many diminutive greenspaces, what later generations would call "vest-pocket" parks. Located in the densely populated tenement districts, these small refuges embodied Vaux's philosophy of democracy in dirt and trees at the neighborhood scale.

Over the decades, Vaux devoted considerable effort to defending the Greensward plan against proponents of unsympathetic alterations and additions. As early as 1863, during Olmsted's absence in California, Vaux successfully thwarted the construction of elaborate neoclassical-style gates that the architect Richard Morris Hunt had proposed for entrances to the park. Columns, statue-topped pillars, and water jets abounded in Hunt's grandiose Francophile designs that he revealed in handsome drawings. Vaux objected to the projects on aesthetic grounds as out of keeping with the simple, pastoral mood of the park landscape. But he also condemned them on the basis of his egalitarian political philosophy. The designs by Hunt, who had studied architecture at the École des Beaux-Arts in Paris, were, he fumed, symbolic of the imperial authoritarianism that Napoleon III maintained over the French.

Nevertheless, Vaux and Olmsted took many lessons from the rebuilding of Paris that proceeded apace under Napoleon III's auspices. "When Louis Napoleon was elected president," writes Esther da Costa Meyer, historian of Second Empire Paris, "he was fired by an ardent wish to modernize Paris. . . . Public parks played an important role in his agenda from the start."[45] Once he had assumed the mantle of emperor, Napoleon III hastened his plans to incorporate many free, accessible greenspaces in the immense rebuilding of Paris directed by Georges-Eugène Haussmann. Under the supervision of Jean-Charles Adolph Alphand, Haussmann's associate, the Bois de Boulogne and the Bois de Vincennes were created, along with other smaller grounds and landscaped squares. Through publications and travel to France (Olmsted met Alphand and visited the Bois de Boulogne eight times in 1859), both Olmsted and Vaux were well aware of the new parks, which took their cue in many respects from the works of Joseph Paxton and the English naturalistic landscape tradition that Napoleon III greatly admired.

The two Americans also learned from Haussmann and Alphand the necessity of incorporating modern principles and means of engineering and sanitation into their park schemes in order to make nature at home in the modern urban environment. Even after the demise of Napoleon III and the Second Empire in 1870, the French park movement continued to progress and hold the attention of others. Vaux objected to the mistaken belief that Paris's parks, squares, and boulevards existed solely because an authoritarian regime had commanded them. He was pleased to note that in the 1878 edition of William Robinson's *Notes on the Parks and Gardens of Paris,* "the author can tell us, by way of comment on this suggestion, that since the establishment of the Republic in France, improvements calculated to produce the best effects on the beauty and salubrity of Paris, have been carried out more vigorously than before, with this difference, that they are done more economically."[46]

Despite his wide knowledge and experience, in his later years Vaux encountered increasing opposition to his professional judgment from those who wished to advance their own proposals for New York's parks. Some opponents turned to Olmsted, whose national prominence overshadowed Vaux's, for support for their particular schemes. Olmsted, however, consistently sided with his old friend. In 1885, when President Grant's widow expressed her wish to have her recently deceased husband interred in New York City, Vaux, as the city's landscape architect, took charge of finding a burial site. He selected a hilltop in Riverside Park, which offered a commanding view of the Hudson River, for what he intended would be a grand mausoleum. After Jacob Wrey Mould, Vaux's longtime assistant in the parks department, hastily designed a temporary tomb there, the chair of the park board expressed doubts about Vaux's site selection and invited Olmsted to come from Brookline to give his opinion on the its appropriateness. Absent from the proceedings, Vaux did not hear his former colleague affirm that "in comparison with any other site that was available, I think the selection made is an admirable one. It is the most suitable spot that could have been found in the city." Furthermore, Olmsted praised it as "a beautiful, noble spot" and commended its selection for such a celebrated purpose.[47]

The last occasion that Olmsted had for supporting his comrade came in 1894, when certain members of parks department board wished to oust Vaux from his position as landscape architect. Their bone of contention lay with the proposed Harlem River Speedway, a grand horse-drawn carriage drive tracing the western bank of the strait connecting the Hudson River with the East River. Vaux, envisioning a design that would conserve the scenic shoreline and cater to pedestrians, found himself at odds with influential board members. They favored an engineer's plan that paid scant attention to the natural scenery and none to making the water's edge accessible to strollers, opting instead for a broad roadway suited to breakneck speeds. Hoping to circumvent Vaux's vigorous attempts to obstruct this plan, the board summoned Olmsted to the city, hoping he would take charge of the project. But Olmsted, known for his decisive stance on matters of his profession, stood firm. He insisted that Vaux was "the most qualified man for this endeavor anywhere in the world." His tone unyielding, Olmsted declared, "It must be understood that unless Mr. Vaux enters into the work with me I will not take it up."[48] Months later, under new leadership, the board reaffirmed Olmsted's endorsement, granting Vaux sole authority over the design of the thoroughfare. Thus, their collaborative vision prevailed, safeguarding both the natural charm of the river edge and the pedestrian's right to enjoy it. New Yorkers benefited from Vaux's intentions until 1919 when the Harlem River Speedway became the present Harlem River Drive.

Another speedway proposition threatened to disturb the tranquility of Central Park at the time when the vegetation had matured as Olmsted and Vaux had envisioned. Thirty-four years after Central Park was begun, the state legislature passed a law authorizing a fast drive within the grounds. Vaux vigorously opposed it. His objections and the efforts of allies eventually defeated the proposal, but the affair alerted the aging Vaux to the vulnerability of his and Olmsted's great creation. The past would need to lay claim on the future. In order to preserve the original spirit of the Greensward plan beyond his time, Vaux decided to groom Samuel Parsons Jr. to succeed him at the Department of Public Parks. He even funded Parsons's employment as superintendent of planting when the city failed to appropriate money for his salary.

Parsons had joined Vaux & Company in 1880 and within a few years had become a partner, along with George K. Radford, a British-trained engineer long resident in New York. Radford had worked with Vaux since the 1870s, taking charge of making topographical surveys for the firm and assisting with business matters. In 1892, however, Radford went out on his own, but by then Downing Vaux had grown into a competent landscape architect and assumed Radford's place. Downing worked together with his father on several projects. But it would be Parsons who carried into the twentieth century the struggle to maintain and keep before the community the original template of Central Park. At Vaux's death in 1895, Parsons succeeded him as landscape architect to the parks department. His mentor's example would continue to exert profound and enduring influence. Vaux, Parsons declared, "has been and always will be for me a potent stimulus to seek to do only good work in the practice of my profession."[49] Until he resigned in 1911, he remained diligently loyal to Vaux and Olmsted's principles throughout the city's park system.

Vaux's troubles over Central Park involved more than defending it from intrusions. Despite his equal role with Olmsted in the design and his subsequent dogged defense of its integrity, he often went unacknowledged in public discussions of the park. Part of the reason was that Olmsted occupied a more prominent position in the public eye than Vaux did. Olmsted was, as Vaux said, the "representative man," not only of their partnership but also of the age: a thoughtful, articulate, and well-connected public intellectual. On one notable occasion in 1879, Vaux's anger at being slighted boiled over. E. L. Godkin, editor of *The Nation,* in an article in the *New-York Tribune* heaped praise on Olmsted as Central Park's designer without mentioning Vaux. In response, Vaux sent a blistering letter to the editor: "I have waited a sufficiently long time," he wrote, "to allow of Mr. Olmsted's disavowal of the greedy misrepresentations made in his behalf by Mr. E. L. Godkin, in regard to the authorship of the designs for the Central and Brooklyn Parks, of which I am the author in every respect, equally with Mr. Olmsted." He continued:

> Consider the case for a moment. Twenty years ago, by taking the first name in our professional partnership relation he became more especially the trustee of our joint artistic property, the Central Park plan, to the conception and execution of which I have devoted the very heart of my life. My efforts during that period toward making the Park what it is are well known to our citizens. I have been throughout loyal to Mr. Olmsted under the most trying circumstances. His representative, Mr. E. L. Godkin, who knows all the

circumstances of the case, has now the repulsively bad faith to step forward publicly and administer our joint estate: To F. L. Olmsted, everything; to C. Vaux, the cut direct."[50]

For Olmsted's part, he always took pains to acknowledge their collaborative efforts. On this occasion, however, he was abroad and unaware of the uproar that Godkin, a friend to both men who should have known better, had stirred up. It fell to Olmsted's stepson Owen to write a letter to the *Tribune* on his father's behalf publicly correcting the record. Godkin himself responded, avowing that any snub had been unintended. Nonetheless, the absence of Vaux's name in tandem with Olmsted's continued throughout his life, and, indeed, persists today.

On several occasions, Vaux rejoined Olmsted to undertake important landscape projects. In the 1870s and 1880s, he supported Olmsted and others in their efforts to preserve and restore the natural scenery at Niagara Falls. The landscape around the famous Cataract had become spoiled with grimy industrial buildings and honky-tonk entertainment attractions. To many, greed had marred and dishonored what was almost considered a sacred site. In 1885 the State of New York returned this land to the ownership of the people when it established the State Reservation at Niagara. Andrew Haswell Green became the head of the commission formed to administer it. Vaux and Olmsted were hired to create a master plan that would restore the battered terrain and organize public access in new ways. The Niagara park was followed in 1888 by Downing Park in Newburgh. On this occasion, the two men worked together pro bono on the design of the park that would honor the memory of America's "Apostle of Taste." The year before, they had teamed up to tackle the redesign of Morningside Park, an extent of challenging acreage located in Upper Manhattan.

Morningside Park was unfinished business from the earlier days of Vaux and Olmsted's association. Back in 1873, they had drawn up the original plan for the long, narrow, ladle-shaped parcel. Their design featured a picturesque area of lagoons with thick plantings overhanging the banks—a scheme that looked forward to Olmsted's 1888 proposal for Buffalo's South Park on Lake Erie. If the city had funded their plan, Vaux would have surely been called upon to design the large conservatory for tropical plants that appeared as part of their intentions. For various reasons, the Morningside Park project languished for fourteen years.

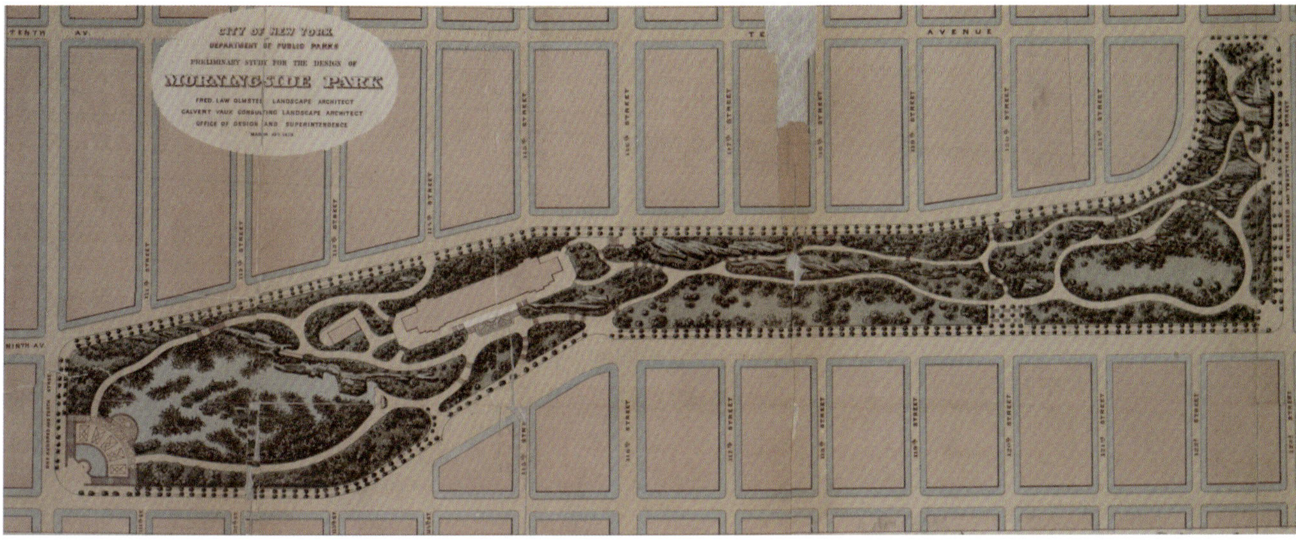

Olmsted and Vaux, *Preliminary Study for the Design of Morningside Park* [1873]. New York Public Library (NYPL) Digital Collections.

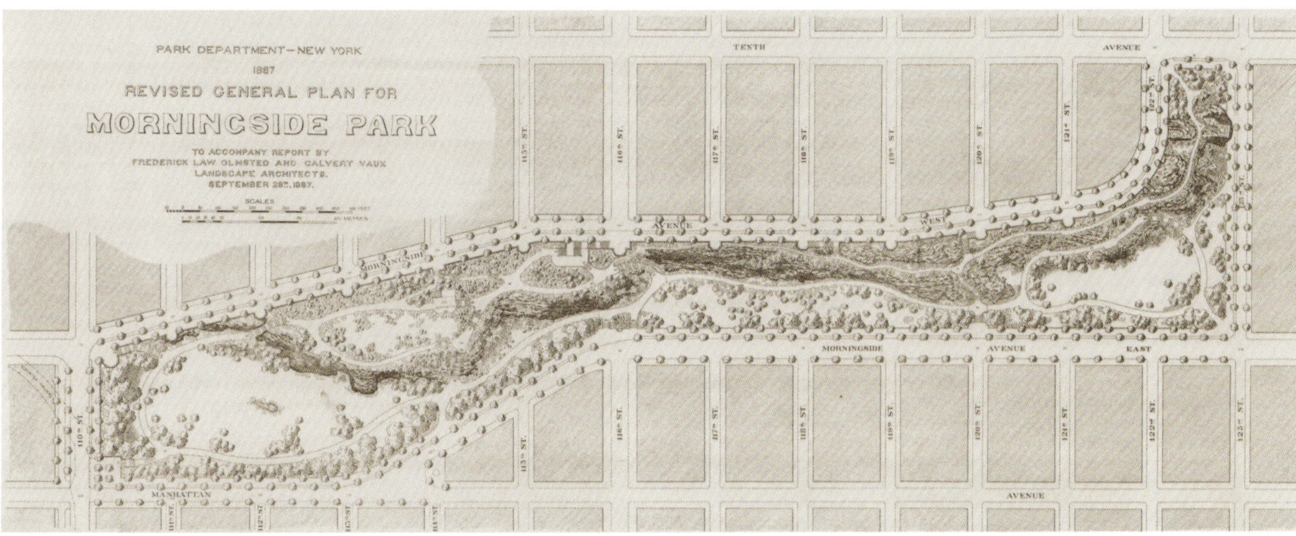

Olmsted and Vaux, *Revised General Plan for Morningside Park,* 1887. Courtesy National Park Service, Frederick Law Olmsted National Historic Site.

Then, as that area was becoming increasingly populated, the city revived it and recalled Olmsted and Vaux to come up with a new design. In their second plan, the partners absented the conservatory and lagoons but developed the clifflike western border along Morningside Avenue as a monumental promenade. Jacob Wrey Mould took responsibility for designing the great ramparts and viewing balconies that were constructed along the new avenue. From here, visitors could enjoy looking at the lower park, the city, and, in the distance, Long Island Sound. They might also come here to watch the sunrise that gave the park its name. It was the last landscape plan for New York City the pair made together.

The final major landscape project that Vaux undertook was for the New York Botanical Garden. In the late 1880s, public-spirited citizens began calling for the establishment of a place in New York City devoted to the scientific study and display of the world's plant life. Certainly Vaux, who had been involved in so many projects to enhance the cultural life of his city, would have agreed with his friend Charles Sprague Sargent, founding director of Harvard's Arnold Arboretum, when he declared in the pages of *Garden and Forest* magazine: "Botanical and zoological gardens form a part, and a very important part, of the educational equipment of a great metropolis; and it is not credible to the people of this city that it is allowed to fall so far behind the other great commercial centres of the world in this respect."[51] His appeal to civic pride invoked the urgency and necessity of the endeavor.

Sargent was one of the members of a committee, which also included Olmsted, charged with identifying a suitable location for the future botanical garden. The committee focused their attention on the 650-acre tract of undeveloped parkland north of the Harlem River newly acquired by the city under the New Parks Act. Approved by the New York State legislature in 1884, the act provided for the purchase of property for future parks in the area north of Manhattan in the Bronx. The site, *Garden and Forest* informed its readers, possessed rare rural beauty:

> Few people of New York know that within their city limits lies one of the most picturesque spots to be found this side of the Adirondacks. . . . It consists of a strip of some two miles long and half a mile wide, mostly wooded, on both banks of the little Bronx River. . . . In some places the river is a narrow stony brook, and in others widens out into placid sheets of water, surrounded with grassy knolls, shaded by tall handsome trees.

Here, merely twenty minutes by train from Grand Central, "the visitor finds no suggestion of a neighboring city beyond an occasional glimpse of gray-coated park watchmen and the shrill echoes of frequent steam-whistles."[52] The new institution would be nestled within 250 acres of this sylvan landscape. Backed by a board of directors that included Andrew Carnegie, J. P. Morgan, and Cornelius Vanderbilt

II, the botanical garden, museum, and arboretum, all modeled on England's Royal Botanic Gardens at Kew, promised to become the finest in the world.[53]

In March 1895 the journal *Park and Cemetery* reported that Calvert Vaux, as landscape architect to the New York City parks department, assisted by Samuel Parsons Jr., had surveyed and studied the botanic garden site. At seventy-one and in failing health, Vaux still maintained a sharp eye for a location's natural advantages. Within the 250 acres situated in "the most beautiful sections of Bronx Park," was the celebrated Hemlock Grove. It was, said Vaux, "the most beautiful natural spot in the entire park System." Vaux directed that this arboreal treasure was to be "absolutely preserved from disturbance in any way whatever."[54]

Once acquainted with the site, Vaux outlined a system of drives and projected locations for future buildings. In this he repeated, for a final time, the method he had established at the beginning of his career: landscape architect preceded architect. In addition to his awareness of natural features, Vaux was attuned to the ways earlier

Entrance to Hemlock Grove, 1912. The LuEsther T. Mertz Library of The New York Botanical Garden.

rural folk had navigated this out-of-the-way place. His circulation plan, notes Gregory Long, president emeritus of New York Botanical Garden, "reflects the old country roads and cow paths that had traversed the site during the nineteenth century."[55]

Vaux's unexpected death in fall 1895 was "a most serious blow" to the members of the botanical garden committee. They readily acknowledged that he "had been very closely associated with them in all of their hopes and plans." Samuel Parsons initially picked up the work, until the parks commissioners decided that "the extended domain and remoteness" of the site presented problems "which can only be solved in the future."[56]

Calvert Vaux distinguished himself from most other architects of his day in the seamless connection he saw between architecture and landscape architecture. In an 1881 article he expressed the hope that more and more practitioners would come to appreciate this relationship. "The two arts are very close together in theory," he stated, "and are destined in the future to be more closely allied in practice." He took heart from the recent example of Paris. "In fact, . . . during the last twenty years," he observed, "[the French] have shown how city architecture can be glorified by judicious planting, and how greensward and trees, shrubs and flowers, may be as pliant in the hands of an artistic designer as wood or stone." For Vaux, the goal of both the landscape architect and the architect was to produce works of art. He defined the goal of this kinship as "desiring to build up a beautiful combination of forms and colors in the open air, in accordance with a pre-conceived design gradually developed out of common materials by the hand labor of others."[57]

At the very beginning of his career, Vaux explained in words and images to readers of *Villas and Cottages* how, together with incorporating innovative modern comforts in his residences, he sought to establish a pleasing relationship between the owner's house and its setting. Property diagrams depicted houses harmoniously sited amid paths, drives, and greenery. Additionally, perspective views, a novel feature in architectural publications at the time, showed buildings residing comfortably in their natural surroundings. Additionally, Vaux devoted consideration to people's enjoyment of the out-of-doors. Scattered throughout his book were drawings for charming garden accessories, including outbuildings, fences, rustic bridges, seats, and gates. Few architectural publications had paid much attention to these supplementary landscape elements.

Vaux described how outward-looking views guided his pen when drawing plans

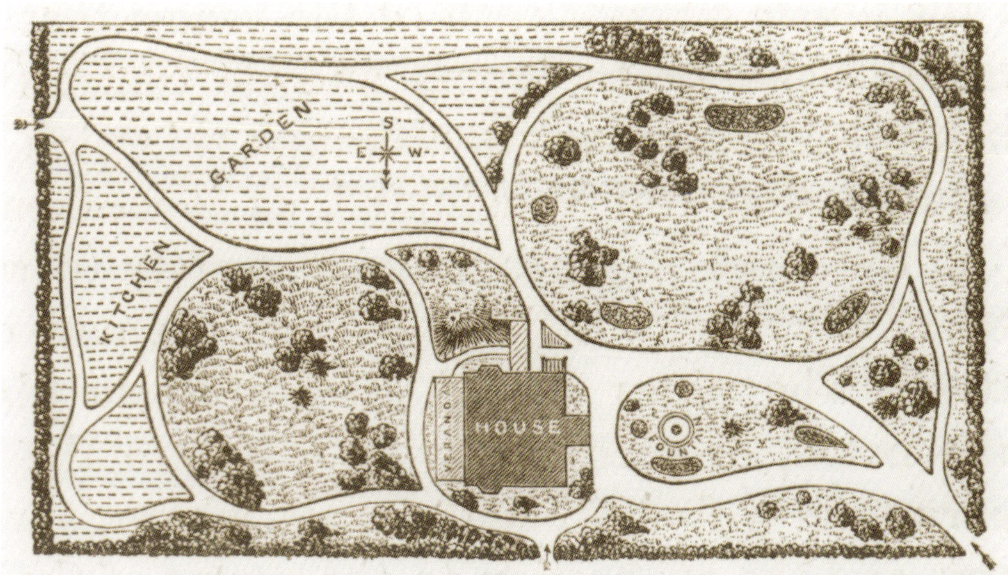

Vaux, "Plan of Grounds." From *Villas and Cottages* (1857).

for dwellings. These took many varied forms in response to the individual site. His riparian home for William Findlay in Newburgh, for example, featured a cross-axial plan that allowed for "an extensive vista . . . through the house" in two directions. The arch of the entrance porch held the view of the Hudson like a picture in a frame, while lateral bay windows overlooked the surrounding lawn. On a Newburgh city lot, Vaux arranged the house of David Moore so that the drawing room windows opened onto "a wide, spacious veranda, commanding an extensive view of the Hudson." For Vaux, "woods, fields, mountains, and rivers *will* be more important than the houses that are built among them."[58] This concept, articulated early in his career, would remain a keystone of Vaux's work throughout his lifetime.

At the start of a new project, Vaux would begin his design process by assessing the site and the surroundings. One of the earliest examples of his working method he described in *Villas and Cottages:*

> The site for the house is on an elevated space of table land. On the veranda front the hillside descends abruptly and picturesquely some sixty or eighty feet within full view of the drive road, and as this steep hillside is well covered with healthy evergreens and fine deciduous trees, it will form, as it were, a broad and handsome base for the house, part of which . . . would be visible from below. On the other side . . . Nature has kindly made ample prepara-

tion . . . for an easy winding road up to the top of the hill. On the south side is a stretch of fine woods, on the edge of which is just the spot for a stable, and scattered here and there among the trees are large boulders of stone, grouped, by accident, . . . quite artistically, and forming pleasant natural seats and nestling-places for ferns and wild flowers.[59]

When he first took on the commission from Lydig and Geraldine Hoyt for a house in Staatsburg, New York, Vaux recounted how he roamed the property until with "due deliberation *pro* and *con,*" he fixed on the most appropriate location for the dwelling. For Nathaniel Parker Willis's residence at Cornwall-on-Hudson, Vaux described how, when he had drawn the initial plans, "the whole design was so fitted among the evergreens, and adapted to every peculiarity of the site, that it appears to be almost surrounded by tall, flourishing trees, although broad stretches of distance in every direction, and extensive views of the river and mountain scenery are gained from the various windows, each view being a separate picture set in a frame of unfading foliage." Another house, across the river in Fishkill, was "situated amidst quiet, agreeable home scenery, and commands several beautiful views, both of the Hudson and of the noble hills that rise up at this point from its eastern shore."[60] Vaux domesticated the pleasure derived from viewing a pleasing prospect.

Moreover, Vaux insisted that the form of his houses comport with their natural context, adapting prominent features, for example, to the peculiarities of the site. "The sky-line of a building," he advised, "should undoubtedly be determined, in a great measure, by the scenery in which it is to be located, and it may be either subdued or picturesque, according to the circumstances of each case"[61] Color, too, played a role in ensuring a snug fit between dwelling and surroundings. Vaux condemned the popular taste for houses painted white with green shutters. "By this means," he complained, "each residence is distinctly protruded from the surrounding scenery, and instead of grouping and harmonizing with it, asserts a right to carry on a separate business on its own account; and this lack of sympathy between the building and its surroundings is very disagreeable to an artistic eye." By contrast, he asserted that "even a harsh, vulgar outline may often pass without particular notice in a view of rural scenery, if the mass is quiet and harmonious in color; while a very tolerable composition may injure materially the views near it if it is painted white."[62]

Nonetheless, to Vaux's fastidious eye, choosing the correct color could be a difficult decision. "It is not sufficient that the various parts of a building should be in proportion to each other," he instructed, "or that it should be, as a whole, harmonious in its actual coloring. It must also possess these qualities when considered with reference to climate, scenery, and surrounding objects." Like a delicate bloom nested in a garden, a work of architecture should be a subtle ornament enhancing rather than detracting from its setting. His counsel was precise: use gray, fawn, and other hues that blended with nature's usual coloring. Moreover, it was "entirely insufficient to use only one or two shades of color for each house." Every rural building required four tints to make it a pleasant object, and he offered specific advice on how to dispose them: "The main walls should be of some agreeable shade of color; the roof-trimmings, verandas, and other wood-work being either of a different color or of a different shade of the same color, so that a contrast, but not a harsh one, may be established. The third color, not widely different from the other wood-work, should be applied to the solid parts of the Venetian blinds, and the movable slats should be painted of the fourth tint."[63]

Around the outside of the house, Vaux cautioned against placing decorative objects and sculpture in the landscape. The admonition applied to both residential and park settings. Contrary to what we today consider the prevailing Victorian taste, Vaux believed that the "copious introduction of architectural ornaments at the salient points about the grounds" seldom produced an agreeable effect.[64] It was distracting to divide our attention between the beauties of art and the beauties of nature—the latter should always take precedence.

In his design for a landscape larger than a garden, Vaux aimed at preserving and augmenting the best existing natural characteristics. He approached each locale with a fresh perspective, taking his cues from how nature had expressed itself at the site. "In every difficult work," he said, "the key-note of success lies, of course, in the idea of thorough subordination, but it must be . . . an industrious, ardently artistic, and sleeplessly active ministry that is constantly seeking for an opportunity to do some little thing to help forward the great result on which Nature is lavishing its powers of creation."[65] He regarded Central Park a prime example of the process. "The object in view all the time was, of course," he said, "the permanent retention of the interesting features of the landscape, and the preservation and emphasis of every natural characteristic of the site." Great practical measures had been taken to achieve this result. "Those who will remember the initial proceedings," he said,

> will call to mind how complicated and apparently iconoclastic they were—the constant need for blasting rock to secure convenient grades for road construction and for efficient drainage, the unintelligible processes of lake

> excavation, the incessant digging and delving necessary for the preparation of the soil, and to adjust the natural surface to the numerous archways demanded by the proposed subway system of roads and walks, all these, and a thousand other necessary incidents of gradual development had to be undertaken in regular sequence, in circumstances disadvantageous to all serenity of appearance, while the works were in process.[66]

Nonetheless, Vaux professed that "an imitation of nature, however successful, is not art." In a park landscape, he said, "the purpose to imitate nature, or to produce an effect which shall seem to be natural, and therefore interesting, is not sufficient." Art depends "on a happy combination of many circumstances that nature, unassisted, is not likely to bring about." The landscape architect must create a harmonious combination of many pleasing elements drawn from nature. The close study of each specific detail and observation of what conditions make "harmonious relations of one, two or more" could yield discovery of "the law of harmonious relation between multitudinous details." If that were put into practice, Vaux concluded, "the result would be a work of art; and the combination of the art thus defined, with the art of architecture, in the production of landscape compositions, is what may properly be denominated landscape architecture."[67]

In Central Park, especially, all efforts were taken to lead unsuspecting visitors into thinking that nothing had been done to modify the evocative terrain they trod. "We cite the Park as an example of the carrying out of the art-idea," asserted the nineteenth-century art critic James Jackson Jarvis, "because, beside a barren site, it owes nothing to nature. Art here has done everything."[68] This was a bit of an overstatement; nonetheless, Vaux was especially proud to tell the story related to him by a friend of Horace Greeley, the influential editor of the *New-York Tribune.* On Greeley's first walk through Central Park, he made no comment, "except just as he was leaving it, when he said with some sense of relief, 'Well they've left it alone better than I thought they would.' "[69]

Calvert Vaux, architect and landscape architect, was well known to artists of the Hudson River School. For a time, Vaux took drawing lessons from the English-born painter Thomas Charles Farrer, who had been a pupil of John Ruskin and espoused his mentor's "truth to nature" philosophy. He often went on sketching trips in the Hudson River Valley with his brother-in-law, the artist Jervis McEntee. (Appreciative of the persuasive power of art, Vaux had asked McEntee to provide images for the Greensward plan so the judges could share his vision of how the raw landscape would look once the design had been implemented and matured.)

As a member of the Century Association, Vaux had opportunities to mix with prominent artists of the day, and he also rented an apartment in the Tenth Street Studio Building, the first in New York designed specifically for artists. Tenth Street Studio was a synergystic gathering of leading painters—Albert Bierstadt, John La Farge, Winslow Homer, William Merritt Chase, and Worthington Whittredge all lived and worked there. Vaux often dined with Whittredge, who later moved to Summit, New Jersey, where he continued his painting career in a house that Vaux had designed for him. Sanford Robinson Gifford, whose light-suffused canvases were compared to J. M. W. Turner's, was also a Tenth Street Studio resident and a friend Vaux enjoyed sketching with in the Catskills.

The most notable of Vaux's Tenth Street Studio associates, however, was Frederic Edwin Church, whose sweeping 1857 painting *Niagara* became an icon of that preeminent natural spectacle. The love for sublime scenic landscape that

Jervis McEntee, *Landscape,* c. 1860s–70s, oil on canvas. Cincinnati Art Museum.

Church expressed in his painting extended also to its preservation, and he was one of the initiators of efforts to rescue Niagara Falls from the grip of commercial and industrial exploitation. In 1870, Church turned to Vaux to help him realize Olana, his exotic dream home at Hudson, New York. While his house was being built, Church served on the Central Park board of commissioners, where he advocated for the ideals embodied in Vaux and Olmsted's Greensward plan.

Worthington Whittredge, *The Trout Pool,* 1870, oil on canvas. Metropolitan Museum of Art. Gift of Colonel Charles A. Fowler, 1921.

Sanford Robinson Gifford, *A Gorge in the Mountains (Kauterskill Clove),* 1862, oil on canvas. Metropolitan Museum of Art. Bequest of Maria DeWitt Jesup, from the collection of her husband, Morris K. Jesup, 1914.

Seeing the natural world as many of his artist friends did, Vaux also came to appreciate the theology of Transcendentalism, especially as preached by Octavius Brooks Frothingham. Frothingham advocated the idea that "man's nature is naturally good and only evil incidentally" and spoke of "a perpetual revelation in the phases of nature," ideas that resonated with Vaux's Anglican education.[70] Vaux

Frederic Edwin Church, *Niagara,* 1857, oil on canvas. Corcoran Collection (Museum Purchase, Gallery Fund).

became a faithful member of Frothingham's radical Unitarian congregation in New York, the "church for the unchurched," and was welcomed into the minister's close circle of friends.

From the moment Vaux first entered the grounds of Downing's Highland Gardens, he embraced the Hudson River Valley landscape as his tutor of nature's lessons. Among his favorite spots was Kaaterskill Falls—the setting of Asher B. Durand's famous tribute to William Cullen Bryant and Thomas Cole, *Kindred Spirits* (1849). Standing at the base of the modest cataract, Vaux described the two-tiered cascade as "so picturesquely grouped in connection with the trees and the rocky precipitous sides of the mountain, that its upper edge, or lip, seen through the spray from below, would appear to be at a great height from the eye." The idyllic scene was, however, marred by "a clumsy boarded structure that has been erected just on the brink of the descent to afford visitors a view clear down into the valley," compromising "the effect that Nature has attempted so successfully to produce," he lamented. (Cole had deleted the offending platform in his paintings of the locale.) Manmade structures, Vaux observed, too often detracted from scenes of natural beauty "through a lack of a little architectural knowledge in a rural way."[71]

Another cherished view he often contemplated was the outlook from the board-and-batten house and studio he designed for Jervis McEntee at Rondout, New York.

Vaux and his family spent many happy times there with the artist and his wife, and Olmsted visited, too. In *Villas and Cottages,* Vaux reproduced the sketch he had made of the snug belvedere and the engaging panorama it commanded of "the most striking and varied description."[72]

The natural wonder of the Palisades, the twenty-mile stretch of sheer cliffs on

Asher B. Durand, *Kindred Spirits,* 1849, oil on canvas. Crystal Bridges Museum of American Art, Bentonville, AR, 2010.106.

the western side of the Hudson across from Upper Manhattan, was another source of inspiration for Vaux and his contemporaries. His friend Sanford Gifford portrayed their majestic beauty in several striking paintings, and Vaux wrote of the cliffs with nuanced observation. "We have first the sky which will have its own individual color and character," he described, "then the cliff which usually contrasts boldly with it, light against dark or dark against light—the space between the horizon and shore line next fills the eye, and it is always sufficiently far off to have a hue of its own, dependent on the day gradated, of course, within itself, but so different from the sky or the cliffs that it makes the impression on the eye, of a distant strip of delicate half tint."[73] His sketch "Restawhile on the Palisades," made in the summer of 1879, depicts a rustic summerhouse perched on the cliff edge, inviting the viewer to stop and contemplate the remarkable scenery.[74] Admiration catalyzed militancy: Vaux was one of the first citizens to advocate for preserving the Palisades from destruction by gravel and stone quarrying interests.

As his depiction of the Palisades reveals, Vaux's appreciation of natural scenery extended beyond the horizon. The sky, he believed, was an often overlooked element of nature and a source of great beauty. "A man who owns an acre of ground cannot look far without reaching its lateral boundaries, but in the direction of the sky, his acre gives him a wide extent of view that constitutes a valuable property," Vaux wrote in his essay "Sky and Sky Line." He went on to reflect that "over half the sky

Vaux, "Design for an Artist's Studio." Courtesy Buffalo & Erie County Public Library.

Sanford Robinson Gifford, *Sunset on the Hudson,* 1876, oil on canvas. Wadsworth Atheneum Museum of Art, The Ella Gallup Sumner and Mary Catlin Sumner Collection Fund, 1958.151.

can be seen from any average acre; and that as its appearance is constantly changing, it becomes practically an almost boundless pictorial possession to a sympathetic observer." Further, he asserted, "the light and color of the sky is the controlling element of beauty in every attractive landscape."[75]

Trees, in Vaux's opinion, played an important role in our comprehension and appreciation of the sky. "By most persons, a tree is conceived as a definite and independent fact of nature," he observed, "its relation to the sky being considered accidental and comparatively unimportant." The human eye, however, naturally perceives both simultaneously, forming a unified impression. The effect could be very pleasing to the viewer. With this in mind, Vaux admonished the landscape architect that "in laying out a country place, large or small, with reference to its landscape attractions, the present and prospective *sky line* is one element of design that needs very skillful attention."[76]

Despite the country's manifest natural beauty, Vaux lamented the lack of aesthetic appeal in America's towns and villages, dismayed by the stark contrast between them and the attractive landscapes they populated. He criticized the majority of town layouts as predictable and "unpicturesque"—"They generally consist of square blocks of houses, each facing the other with conventional regularity," he observed. "This arrangement is so discordant with the varied outlines characterizing American scenery that Dame Nature refuses, at the outset, to have anything to do with them, and they never seem afterward to get any better acquainted with her."[77] To remedy the situation, Vaux advised following the "well-balanced irregularity" found in nature:

> Human nature, when allowed a free, healthy scope, loves heartily this well-balanced irregularity, and longs for it in life, in character, and in almost every thing. . . . We want far less formality and restraint in the plans of our new villages. The roads should wind in graceful, easy curves, and be laid out in accordance with the formation of the ground and the natural features of interest. A single existing tree ought often to be the all-sufficient reason for slightly diverting the line of a road, so as to take advantage of its shade, instead of cutting it down and grubbing up its roots."[78]

Vaux, "Design for a Rustic Shelter" ("Restawhile on the Palisades"), 1879.
From Alexander F. Oakey, *Home Grounds* (1881).

One notable exception Vaux admired was Middletown, Connecticut. Although it was not large, Vaux observed in 1857, it possessed "a cheerful and very fascinating rural character." This he attributed in large measure "to the attention that has been bestowed, from time to time, to planting in the streets and avenues." The town could be grateful to those who first decided to line the streets with "a judicious selection of specimens," for those earlier efforts "have, without doubt, been mainly instrumental in giving to the whole town that refined rural character that makes it now so desirable a place of residence." The transient visitor, remarked Vaux, "can hardly fail to be struck with the number of fine, flourishing specimens of the different varieties of shade trees that court his attention when passing through the various avenues."[79]

Similarly, he admired Newburgh's Grand Street for its "beautiful elms and maples, with their wide-spreading and interacting branches." Running high above and parallel with the river, the leafy residential thoroughfare offered the visitor "often-recurring glimpses of the Hudson, with its gleaming and ever-shifting freight of sails that one catches at intervals framed in the foliage of the trees on the side-streets." The vignettes lent the place "a charming pictorial character that is very rarely attainable."[80]

Regarding the domestic architecture of small towns, Vaux, the partisan of republican values, took heart that "almost every store-keeper and mechanic can contrive, even when quite young, to buy his own lot and live in his own house." Yet, he bemoaned the disappointing level of national taste as expressed in its ordinary houses: "Each of these bare, bald, white cubes tells its monotonous story of a youth passed with little or no cultivation of the higher natural perceptions." He blamed "a system of education in which the study of the beautiful, in its most simple elements, is neglected, and apparently despised."[81] This he saw manifested in the general aspect of the local schoolhouse itself. This building, "in which the earliest and most active germs of progressive thought are commenced," had no lessons to teach its impressionable occupants. It was more often than not "a naked, shabby structure, without a tree or a shrub near it," which was remarkable "chiefly for an air of coarse neglect that pervades its whole aspect."[82]

It was a sentiment that his friend Olmsted shared. And like Olmsted, Vaux saw the absence of aesthetic appreciation as a deficiency in the American character. "The lack of taste perceptible all over the country," Vaux wrote as early as 1855, "is a weakness that affects the whole bone and muscle of the body-politic."[83] It was his hope that institutions such as the Metropolitan Museum of Art, the National Sculpture Society, the National Academy of Design, and other cultural organizations he actively supported would improve the situation, and he maintained faith in the press as a great national educator.

Vaux also attributed the general lack of good design in America in large part to the tendency of people to undervalue the services of design professionals. On coming to the United States, he had discovered that the "system of remuneration" for architects and landscape designers was "defective and unsettled." At the back of his 1857 edition of *Villas and Cottages,* he published his terms for designing a dwelling. For plans and specifications, he required 2.5 percent; for detail drawings, 1 percent; and for superintendence, 1.5 percent, for a total of 5 percent. This schedule of fees, he stated, was "the usual commission of architects." As he later affirmed to Olmsted, "I refused all business not in the plan I determined on."[84] He soon joined others in a group of New York architects who began meeting in 1857 to establish professional standards. Constituting themselves as the American Institute of Architects, they adopted the scale of charges that Vaux had printed in his book.

Vaux likewise promoted the need for strict contractual agreements for landscape design projects. Early on in his relationship with Olmsted, he felt obliged to chide his partner for offering prospective clients too much advice before securing a firm financial agreement. There were other lessons to be learned in their fledgling profession. After making the mistake of taking land for compensation when they laid out the residential suburb of Riverside, the partners specified a fee based on acreage, using terms similar to those for architects. Ironically, for all the sound business advice Vaux gave to Olmsted, it would be Olmsted who, in later years, became the head of a nationally eminent design firm. Following a downturn in his architectural endeavors in the late 1870s, Vaux struggled to hold pace with Olmsted's success as a landscape architect. During the last years of his life, Vaux succeeded in achieving only middling financial success. His private practice limped far behind that of his friend in Brookline. Vaux came to depend primarily on his salary from the Department of Public Parks to keep himself afloat economically. Nevertheless, above all else, Vaux consistently championed the professional recognition of his craft.

After Vaux's death, his son Downing and Samuel Parsons Jr. continued his efforts to establish landscape architecture as a bona fide discipline. In 1899, after Parsons had worked for several years to organize a permanent professional body, the two joined with nine others, including Olmsted's stepson John C. Olmsted and Frederick Law Olmsted Jr., to found the American Society of Landscape Architects (ASLA). Parsons, whose office hosted the organization's first meeting, served as president from 1905 to 1907; Downing Vaux functioned as secretary from 1900 to

1909. Bremer W. Pond, chronicler of the early years of the ASLA, credited Downing Vaux with being "largely responsible for keeping the young organization alive through this first decade."[85] As the historian Joy Kestenbaum has noted, Downing continued his father's efforts on behalf of professional standing, advocating for full collaboration among architects, engineers, and landscape architects from the outset of the design process.[86]

On November 21, 1895, the New York press reported that Calvert Vaux had gone missing while staying at the home of his son Bowyer in the new suburban seaside resort of Bensonhurst in Brooklyn. An avid canoer—in 1886 he won the first New York Canoe Club International Challenge Cup—Bowyer lived near Coney Island Creek, a popular venue with boaters. Vaux, whose wife Mary had died a few months earlier in a carriage accident, had arrived at Bowyer's a few days before to recuperate from a condition described as "nervous prostration." Fond of walking to the nearby shore to view the sunset over the ocean, he had failed to return from his stroll the previous day. Later, his body was found floating in the choppy waters of Gravesend Bay. The family disputed speculation that he had taken his own life. "He was always cheerful and there was nothing in either his professional or domestic relations to give him the slightest uneasiness," Bowyer reported. "It is my belief that my father, who was nearsighted and somewhat feeble, simply stumbled into the bay while watching Tuesday's sunset from one of the Bensonhurst piers."[87] The truth was never determined, but dark moods followed the family thereafter. Vaux's son Downing and daughter Julia both died by their own hands.

By fall 1895, Olmsted's mind had been failing for some time, prompting his family to delay breaking the news of Vaux's drowning until several months later. Three years after Olmsted's death in 1903, Samuel Parsons took stock of his mentor's historic partnership with Olmsted:

> The association of these two remarkable men was, for the public and the art of the landscape architect in this country, most happy. Holding identical views as to the underlying principles of the art, in temperament and training each supplemented the other admirably. Vaux, notwithstanding his training as an architect, saw nature with the eyes and from the point of view of a painter of landscape, whose art, in spare moments, he assiduously practiced. . . . Of a shy and retiring disposition, his difficulties in written and

William Merritt Chase, *Gravesend Bay (The Lower Bay),* 1889, pastel on paper. ARTGEN/Alamy Stock Photo.

> spoken language were many and great, although he wrote much of value. His means of expression being limited to his art, he mastered it the more thoroughly through stress of necessity, while the fluent eloquence of his associate left him freer to follow it.[88]

At Central Park and later at Prospect Park in Brooklyn, Vaux had sought out Olmsted to join him, even telling his friend he could not take on the Brooklyn job without him. Vaux ceded the administrative and public aspects of their partnership to Olmsted. He relied on Olmsted to represent and help him articulate their shared ideals, wishing to focus primarily on design and aesthetics. Parsons, who in some ways filled Olmsted's place in Vaux's later career, astutely observed that while Olmsted was "a leader of men, a man of magnetism and charm, a literary genius," he was "hardly the creative artist that Mr. Vaux was." Moreover, he declared, just as Olmsted, the more extroverted personality, saw poetry in broad landscape effects, "there was an intimate and subtle quality to Mr. Vaux's work at its best that we scarcely find elsewhere, not in Repton, Pückler or Olmsted."[89]

Influenced by a library of theoretical and practical writing on landscape, the evocative artworks of the Hudson River School, and the pantheistic beliefs of American Transcendentalism, Calvert Vaux forged a philosophy of landscape architecture that was rooted in the natural world. "Mr. Vaux was profoundly in love with Nature," stated Parsons, "and endeavored to study and comprehend her in all her moods."[90] "Having studied carefully the works and the method of working of the Creator," Vaux wrote a statement that might have served as his guiding principle: "The designer of a landscape can bring into successful play the great forces of Nature, and subordinating his own personality, can secure for his work an undying vitality which can only follow from such a direct reliance on the resources of the Infinite."[91]

At the time of Vaux's death, his longtime associate Andrew Haswell Green fondly remembered him to his fellow members of the board of the Department of Public Parks. Green recalled that he had known Vaux for thirty years, "for twelve or fifteen of them in almost daily conference," and asserted that Vaux "had no peer" as a landscape architect. "In the construction of the Central Park in its varied artistic arrangements for the popular pleasure," Green wrote, "his, above all others, was the master mind and guide." He went on to add a heartfelt endorsement of his colleague's character and contributions:

> To his early thorough professional training in architecture, he added a rare genius for landscape treatment. . . . Devoted to his profession, he always kept strictly within its lines. He entertained no jealousies, no rivalries. He forbore from personal controversy, but came to the front resolutely and courageously to defend the public interests entrusted to his care, regardless of the influences arrayed against him. . . . Time fails me for more than a brief allusion to the great public service rendered by this most modest, upright, and able [member] of the profession that he adorned.[92]

In closing his tribute, Green expressed the hope that measures would soon be taken to ensure that Vaux's memory would be honored in a manner befitting his service to his city and his profession. One hundred years later, in 1998, the City of New York created Calvert Vaux Park at the site on Gravesend Bay where he had died.

Lake fog, Central Park. Photo by Sara Cedar Miller, courtesy Central Park Conservancy.

PROJECTS

Over the course of his career, Calvert Vaux designed, independently or collaboratively, a great range of landscapes of varying scale and complexity, including estate grounds, rural cemeteries, urban parks, and institutional campuses. Many of his designs no longer exist; others are so altered that they no longer convey his conception. In deciding which among Vaux's extant works to include here, I considered the project's significance in the context of the early days of the profession. I also aimed to illustrate the scope of his work, and importantly, showcase his artistic genius.

“The Point, Staatsburg, N.Y.,” postcard. Courtesy Staatsburg Library Postcard Collection.

Lydig and Geraldine Hoyt House / The Point, Staatsburg, NY

(1855)

When Vaux featured in *Villas and Cottages* the large country house overlooking the Hudson River he designed in 1855 for Lydig and Geraldine Hoyt at Staatsburg, New York, he opened the discussion wearing his landscape architect's hat. Roaming their extensive farmland, he found it difficult "to select an elevated situation commanding the best views," but eventually he identified the optimal site, one that offered a panorama of the Hudson and the Catskills he found "in every respect delightful." The site was, however, limited in size and varied in surface. Vaux also noted that it was located on a part of the property that was "entirely covered by a handsome growth of trees." This attractive grove he was determined "to preserve uninjured as far as was compatible with a convenient arrangement of the plan."[1] Vaux's challenge was to integrate the house artfully into the restrictive setting while maximizing the fine natural scenery it had to offer.[2]

The Hoyts were ideal clients for Vaux. Lydig was a sharp Wall Street lawyer whom a friend described as also possessing a poetic nature. Blanche Geraldine, née Livingston, descended from a venerable Hudson River Valley family. People knew her as a woman whose "practical sense and shrewdness were constantly displayed in the works of charity to which she devoted herself."[3] After ten years of married life in New York, the couple decided to move with their family of five children to the country. In 1852 they bought sixty-two acres of farmland fifty miles north of Manhattan near to Geraldine's ancestral home. Two years later, Blanche Geraldine's mother gave them an additional twenty-nine acres adjacent to the original purchase. (Whether Vaux suggested adding the waterfront land to their property or it was Blanche Geraldine's idea, given her familiarity with its attractions from her childhood, remains uncertain.) This parcel projected out into the river where it made a sharp bend, a situation that prompted the Hoyts to name their place The Point. The site was also a half mile distant from the noise and smoke of the railroad that generally followed the river's eastern shoreline. It was on this out-of-the-ordinary spot that Vaux chose to locate their new house, the plans for which are dated 1855.

Vaux took special pains with the arrangement of the house interior to capitalize on the splendid views, an effort epitomized by the spacious dining room. Here, he lined the west wall with generously proportioned floor-to-ceiling windows, affording diners a full view of the picturelike panorama. Of a summer evening, with the windows opened, visitors might step through this natural scenic wallpaper onto a wide terrace where, sheltered beneath a permanent canopy in the open air, they could admire the majestic vista of river and mountains. To ensure that so fine a prospect was continuous, Vaux secured the terrace roof by means of overhead chains, eliminating the need for supporting posts. (He included a similar covered terrace in his plan for the Federico Barreda residence in Newport, Rhode Island, where residents could enjoy unobstructed views of the ocean.) Vaux took other steps to adapt the architectural arrangements to the landscape, including placing the kitchen in the basement, a practice he generally avoided, to provide a second prospect from the north side of the building.

Vaux's layout of the grounds continued his desire to adapt the house to its surroundings. Those approaching from the public highway were directed along an extended drive following the contours of the land. Upon reaching the house, they glimpsed it nestled in a grove of mature forest trees. Vaux aimed for a picturesque treatment of the area around the dwelling, noting, "The ground was so irregular and broken that it seemed judicious to aim at a varied outline and picturesque effect in the immediate vicinity of the house, rather than to attempt smooth extents of lawn on a level, or nearly so, with the principal floor." The house itself mirrored this aesthetic, being described by Vaux as a "picturesque" villa, with high peaked roofs, hooded dormers, verge-boarded gables, and a Gothic-arched porch entrance. The variety of outline and detail were evocative of its surroundings.[4]

For materials, Vaux chose native bluestone quarried nearby on the Hoyts' ninety-one-acre farm. He predicted that in fifteen or so years, this granite-hard stone would assume "a delicate, luminous gray tint, each stone differing just so much from the one next to it as to give life and brilliancy to the general effect in the sunlight." In Vaux's estimation the homegrown masonry harmonized beautifully with the land-

Front entrance, Hoyt House, n.d. Piersaull Collection, Franklin D. Roosevelt Library, Hyde Park, #43-183-56.

scape and was, "in connection with the landscape, . . . far more beautiful in color than any brown stone, marble, or brick."[5] All in all, the house and its setting presented an image in which nature held sway.

For over a century, the descendants of Lydig and Blanche Geraldine enjoyed this comfortable and picturesque country house. In 1962 the State of New York acquired the property as part of Norrie State Park, granting public access to The Point's splendid natural setting and scenic views. However, the new owner disregarded the architectural and landscape value of this remarkable estate. The dwelling fell into disrepair, and the grounds became overgrown, obscuring the once picture-perfect views with vegetation. At one time, authorities even considered demolishing Vaux's masterwork to make way for a swimming pool. In 2007, however, concerned citizens formed the Calvert Vaux Preservation Alliance to halt the deterioration and restore the house and grounds to their former beauty. The Point is now included as part of the Hudson River Historic District in the National Register of Historic Places.

View in the Ravine. Photo by Sara Cedar Miller, courtesy Central Park Conservancy.

Central Park, Manhattan

(1858–1895; with F. L. Olmsted)

It is a fundamental truth, as both Vaux and Olmsted often asserted, that the plan they developed as their entry in the 1858 competition resulted from a seamless collaboration. Neither man could claim precedence over the other in the work. Despite this, many later commentators would lose sight of Vaux's essential contribution.

Working late into many nights at Vaux's home on Eighteenth Street, the pair meticulously crafted a portfolio they submitted to the jury under the name "Greensward," a reference to the large open areas of lawn their plan included and its pastoral ambience. Surely it was Vaux who drew the complex sepia ink plan on the 27-by-123-inch strip of paper the partners entered as submission no. 33 and is now preserved in the New York City Municipal Archives. Of the two men, Vaux alone possessed requisite skills of a professional architectural draftsman—a function he had brought to Downing's office years earlier—together with proficiency in lettering maps, which he had acquired back in England to earn extra money.

Samuel Parsons Jr., Calvert Vaux's close friend and associate, furnished us a brief glimpse into those heady days when the two were thrashing out their ideas and committing them to paper. "Mr. Vaux enjoyed relating many incidents of their protracted studies of the 'Greensward' plan," he recalled in 1919. "They wrestled weeks and months to solve the difficult problems involved. Many were the discussions and even battles in defense of their views, for the problems were difficult and complicated. There were hills to make higher, morasses and gullies to fill up, or make deeper, as the case might be, always keeping carefully in view the ultimate effect years hence."[1] With consummate artistry, they coaxed recalcitrant topography into a semblance of

Plan of the Central Park, City of New York, 1860. Courtesy Municipal Archives, City of New York.

a pastoral landscape, a "country park," the fictive setting of a far-off rural domain in the clasp of a bustling city. Somewhat to their surprise, their harmonious fusion of nature and artistry won out over some thirty-two other competitors.

If modern-day visitors to Central Park could go on a tour of the grounds with Olmsted and Vaux as their guides, these collaborators would tell them that the landscape they created was meant to be an artistic facsimile of nature in its gentler moods. Olmsted spoke for both of them when he defined the "landscape character of a park" as

> that of an idealized, broad stretch of pasture, offering in its fair, sloping surfaces, dressed with fine, close herbage, its ready alternatives of shade with sunny spaces, and its still waters of easy approach, attractive promises in every direction, and, consequently, invitations to movement on all sides, go through it where one may. Thus the essential qualification of a park is *range,* and to the emphasizing of the idea of range in a park, buildings and all artificial constructions should be subordinated.[2]

In their minds, the park was to be an idyllic refuge of fields, woods, streams, and lakes amid the bustling city. Vaux, with Olmsted, believed that especially an open meadow possessed outsized power to impart a feeling of liberation and well-being. In its way, nature would work its renewing magic on the wearied spirits of city dwellers. "Hill and dale, wood and water, grass and green leaves," they asserted, "are the natural food and refreshment of the human eye—an organ of sense so delicately adjusted as to require something more than dull colors and

New York City, seen from the Green, 1868, attr. H. A. Ferguson. Library of Congress Prints and Photographs Division.

uninteresting forms, and is but little ministered to, in a pleasant way, in the portion of the city devoted to plain, straight-forward business or even domestic routine."[3] And to prevent the sights and sounds of the city from disturbing visitors' enjoyment of the park, Vaux and Olmsted planted trees and thick foliage that served as a green curtain drawn along its borders.

The landscape that they were given to work with—their unprepared canvas—was in fact far from blank, however. As the historian Sara Cedar Miller notes, "On the land where Central Park is today there were once businesses, churches, farms, burial grounds, the island's first major post road to the mainland, residents of the Motherhouse and school of the Sisters of Charity of Mount St. Vincent, and approximately 200 households."[4]

Topographically, the land naturally divided itself into southern and northern portions, each presenting unique challenges and opportunities for enhancement. The southern or lower part of the park—the area south of Seventy-Ninth Street—posed the greatest problems in converting nature's raw material into a finished artistic product. "When the park was begun," wrote Edward Hagaman Hall, the early historian of New York City who grew up with the park, "there were casual observers who thought the selection of the site an unfortunate one because its gen-

"View of house and surrounding fields," 1862[?]. Photo by Victor Prevost. NYPL Digital Collections.

eral ruggedness was regarded as being forbidding, rather than expressive of dignity or grace. But the impression was due to the absence of soil and foliage at that time; and as the lacking elements were supplied, the quality of picturesqueness became agreeably prominent."[5]

Achieving the desired effect required a great deal of earth moving, blasting, damming, planting, and general rearrangement of the surface. Among the most dramatic changes to the face of the land were the creation of the twenty-acre lake just north of the carriage drive at Seventy-Second Street and the transformation of the barren hillside beyond it into the picturesque woodland known as the Ramble. Additionally, the designers grappled with two large reservoirs that lay adjacent to each other above Seventy-Ninth Street. (The smaller of the two was drained in 1931 to create the present Great Lawn and Turtle Pond.)

Beyond the reservoirs, nature endowed the northern portion of the park with more varied scenery than it had bestowed to the south. Olmsted and Vaux focused here on making accessible what already existed. Names such as the Pool, the Loch, the Ravine, the Great Hill, the North Woods, the Harlem Meer, and the North Meadow exemplify the picturesque elements that the landscape architects subtly improved and made reachable through a wandering network of footpaths and carriage roads. The roll call of features reads like a table of contents to a volume of pastoral verses. Perhaps these quaint park locations, which convey a decidedly British country flavor, were dreamed up mostly by the Englishman Vaux, for he had a poetical turn of mind.

How do we distinguish Vaux's contributions to Central Park from Olmsted's? The genesis of the park design is owed to Vaux's influence: his dissatisfaction with the original plan, which led him to promote a competition; his invitation to Olmsted to join him in preparing an entry; his decision to hire Jervis McEntee to prepare oil sketches to illustrate the Greensward plan for the judges. In addition to his keen aesthetic sense, Vaux brought to the enterprise practical experience from his work with Downing. Andrew Haswell Green credited him with the innovative concept of sinking the four transverse roads called for in the competition—one of

Jervis McEntee, *View in Central Park,* 1858, oil on canvas. The New York Historical.

Greensward Presentation board no. 5 (view of the Lake from Vista Rock), 1858. Courtesy Municipal Archives, City of New York.

"View in Central Park," n.d. NYPL Digital Collections.

the most distinctive features of the Greensward plan.[6] Unlike the level street crossings in Downing's Washington park plan which Vaux knew well, these below-grade east–west connectors ensured that visitors could enjoy the tranquil landscape undisturbed by city traffic.

Because much of the work in the northern section came about in later years, when Vaux was more closely associated with the park than Olmsted, he may well have had the greater hand in articulating that area. "Before he died," Samuel Parsons attested, "Mr. Vaux had planned almost every detail for the final accomplishment of the work." Yet, even so, Vaux did not live long enough to see the park finished as he had envisioned it. In 1910, "after some fifty-seven years of effort on the part of citizens, superintendents, landscape architects, and commissioners," Parsons, then superintendent of the park, noted that significant parts remained unfinished. These, he said, were "the territories from 79th Street to 86th Street, east side; from 96th Street to 100th Street, east side; all along the west side from 110th to 100th Street and from 81st Street to 77th Street"[7]

From Parson's account, we also know that lush foundation plantings at the

“A romantic spot, Central Park,” 1899.
Library of Congress Prints and Photographs Division.

“Lady Cycling, Central Park,” 1896.
Library of Congress Prints and Photographs Division.

"Group in Central Park," n.d. Library of Congress Prints and Photographs Division.

entrance to Vaux's vine-clad Casino were from his plans, as were flower beds that once ornamented the base of the Arsenal. Their layered strata demonstrated one of Vaux's principles of garden design, that

> everywhere the same laws of design should control—the low, broad, or narrow plantations in contrast or contradiction with high ones. In the beds of flowers the heights of the plants should bear the same relation to each other in the garden as grass spaces and trees and shrubs in the park; alternately making, as it were, the grass space, and then coleus and canna, for the trees and shrubs. It is not so much a question of the kind of plants as their mode

"View of the crossing in connection with 8th Ave. and 96th St.," 1862. Photo by Victor Prevost. NYPL Digital Collections.

"Observatory and Tunnel, west side," n.d. NYPL Digital Collections.

"The Casino—Central Park." From *Treat's Illustrated New York, Philadelphia and surroundings* (1876).

> of treatment. The law, the principle, the type should be the same in all cases. The unity of effect is just as important as the variety.[8]

Vaux could also claim credit for the many architectural features, such as bridges, summerhouses, covered seats, and various other structures, that their plans called for. In his mandate, however, architecture, whatever form it took or function it served, was to exist under the condition of "subordination" to the pastoral spirit that ruled the Greensward plan. The most architecturally rich park that Olmsted and Vaux would design, Central Park tested Vaux's skills as an architect who decreed that the landscape reign over architecture.

Chief among Vaux's Central Park structures was the Terrace (more commonly known today as Bethesda Terrace, after Emma Stebbins's monumental Bethesda Angel statue), which, according to Vaux, was centrally located to supply the dominant feature lacking in the geology of the park. Situated at the level of Seventy-Second Street, the grand Terrace would be the place toward which park goers would gravitate. Here, on its ramps, balustrades, and piers, Jacob Wrey Mould lavished his artistic imagination on designs of carvings that celebrate the four seasons. Like the terraces attached to the garden side of large country houses, it would also mark the transition from the formal promenade of the Mall to the natural park surroundings. Visitors were invited to linger and contemplate the extensive landscape composition that Olmsted and Vaux had created: the broad lake, the verdantly planted hillside of the Ramble on the opposite shore, and the distant parkland to the north. "In one sense," the architectural critic Paul Goldberger has asserted, "this is as romantic a place as there is in the park—an intricate terrace and fountain, set into a natural landscape as a springboard to a view."[9]

Wide staircases eased passage to the lower level esplanade, at the center of which a large circular fountain was graced by Stebbins's *Angel of the Waters.* Commissioned by the park board and installed in 1873, the winged figure reminded a more biblically conscious age that pure water was a heavenly gift to humanity. From here, various pathways invite people to venture farther into the park or to the boathouse, where they might enjoy refreshments or rent a boat for a leisurely row on the water. "Here I would let the New Yorker feel that the richest man in New York or elsewhere cannot spend as freely . . . just for his lounge," Vaux told a friend of his creation.[10]

"Terrace, fountain and lake, Central Park—a 'breathing place' of the great metropolis," 1902. Library of Congress Prints and Photographs Division.

"The Lake from the east side," n.d. NYPL Digital Collections.

"A quiet spot in Central Park," 1909. Library of Congress Prints and Photographs Division.

"Rustic rest, Central Park," n.d. Library of Congress Prints and Photographs Division.

The second major structure that Vaux contributed to the park landscape was the Belvedere. This Romanesque-style rusticated stone pavilion, open to the elements, rests firmly on the large rock outcropping that marks the highest point in the park. The Belvedere, as the name implies, was to be a place where visitors might enjoy extensive views of the park, both north and south. Vaux knew that towers had provided owners of large private grounds in his native England with the pleasure of casting their gaze over a wide prospect of scenery. Vaux democratized this innate human pleasure. At the Belvedere, the art historian Kerry Dean Carso has observed, "people of all social classes were able to experience the delight in elevation and the power inherent in the view from above."[11]

Vaux designed the Dairy for the convenience of park visitors, especially younger ones. Tucked away on the side of a hill, the highly picturesque building was a place where mothers could bring their children for fresh milk, a luxury for many who had no access to it let alone ever seen or touched a real cow. (One was kept tethered nearby.) Youngsters might also play on the expansive lawn in front, where toys and equipment could be borrowed for the afternoon.[12] Today, the colorful building attracts a different clientele as the Central Park Conservancy's official visitor center.

"The Dairy," n.d. NYPL Digital Collections.

Vaux, *Study for Belvedere – South Elevation*, 1867. Courtesy Municipal Archives, City of New York.

As walking was considered the preferred way of experiencing the park, Olmsted and Vaux, to keep pedestrian traffic safe from carriages and equestrians, designed a circulation system they described as the "separation of ways." The idea originated with British landscape architect Joseph Paxton, in his design for Prince's Park in Liverpool, an early public park that pioneered several elements found in the Greensward plan. Completed in 1844, "the project enabled Paxton to try out ideas he had been developing for years," observes the historian Kate Colquhoun, "in particular, the making of a clear distinction between vehicular and pedestrian traffic, the inclusion of water in the overall plan, the landscaping of open meadow, . . . wide views and winding paths."[13] Paxton further advanced this concept in his much admired park at Birkenhead, a place that Olmsted had visited on his 1850 tour of England, which greatly influenced his thinking about public parks and was probably the true inspiration for the idea of the "separation of ways" in Central Park. Acknowledging Vaux and Olmsted's debt to Birkenhead, George Chadwick, in his study of Paxton's works, affirmed that "Central

Park exhibits the most completely articulated system of circulation of any public park before or since."[14] In Prince's Park and in his later park designs, Paxton had also shown Olmsted and Vaux how to fashion a carriage drive that snaked around the site's perimeter and to screen the park from the surrounding town with a wall of green.

Keeping pedestrian paths, bridle paths, and carriage drives separate from one another called for the construction of bridge overpasses throughout the Central Park landscape. Vaux's charming structures allowed visitors to amble in the landscape without fear of encountering a carriage or equestrian. The art critic Clarence Cook, who wrote the first book devoted to an American municipal park, remarked that before Central Park few bridges in this country merited close attention for their

Springbanks Arch, c. 1865. Library of Congress Prints and Photographs Division.

Balcony Bridge, c. 1865. Library of Congress Prints and Photographs Division.

beauty. "For the most part," Cook declared, "our bridges are as ugly as engineers, with their dryasdust brains, can devise. But in the Park the effort was made to have the bridges not only solidly built, but as elegantly, and in as great variety of designs, as could be contrived. They are built of stone, of brick, of iron, and of these materials in combination."[15] Vaux shunned the utilitarian blueprints that engineers had devised for spanning the continent's rivers and railways. The many bridges and viaducts he devised for Central Park constitute the finest collection of such structures in any American park landscape.

As Cook had noted, for his bridge designs, Vaux used a medley of forms and materials. Some, the Ramble Arch and Huddlestone Arch, for example, are composed of worn, rusticated stone or immense boulders. For the Balcony Bridge, with its twin polygonal projecting stone bays that invite visitors to stop and regard the scenery, and the Denesmouth Arch, Vaux employed carefully dressed stone. The red-and-yellow-banded brick Playmates Arch indulged the popular Victorian taste for multicolored materials, which Mould had introduced to America with his 1853 design for All Souls Unitarian Church. Others, notably the elegant Bow Bridge, which spans an arm of the lake in a single graceful leap, exploit the ductile prop-

"View in the Ramble," n.d. NYPL Digital Collections.

"Rustic Arch in the Ramble," c. 1865. Library of Congress Prints and Photographs Division.

“Bow Bridge, Spanning Lake,” n.d. Library of Congress Prints and Photographs Division.

erties of iron. Some, such as the Oak Bridge, are sturdy structures of finely crafted wood. Vaux’s most picturesque bridges are those in a rustic style. Especially suited to the wilder setting of the Ramble, these simple, rugged crossings consist of locally harvested cedar logs.

In most instances, Vaux planted shrubs and vines to assimilate these structures into their surroundings. “The entrance and exit to a bridge should be clothed and screened with foliage,” Samuel Parsons explained. “The bridge should emerge from the foliage with a certain distinction and yet not obtrusively.”[16] Springbanks Arch in the quiet reaches of the northern park exemplifies Vaux’s adeptness in tailoring bridges to their surroundings. Walkers on the pedestrian path along the spring’s edge through the archway remained oblivious to the bridle path above, concealed behind lush vegetation.

The rustic style also prevailed for structures large and small that Vaux designed for more out-of-the-way parts of the park landscape. These provided visitors with numerous places of rest and retreat. The immense Kinderberg (Dutch for "children's mountain") arbor was the grandest of them all. Completed in 1868, its forest of trunks and branches enclosed a hilltop near Sixty-Fifth Street (since 1952 the site of the Chess & Checkers House), where many young visitors and their guardians came for rest and recreation. Ample built-in seating and numerous tables for games enhanced their leisure. The fanciful Umbrella Structure sheltered a bench in the Ramble commanding a pretty view of Bow Bridge and the lake. The rustic country structures were a charming embodiment of the Greensward plan, transporting park visitors far away from the city.[17]

Central Park, Vaux maintained, should provide the citizens of New York with

"Gothic Arch, Spanning bridlepath," n.d. Library of Congress Prints and Photographs Division.

"Gothic Arch, detail of cast-iron gothic motifs," n.d. Library of Congress Prints and Photographs Division.

three vital things: "First, air, purified by abundant foliage. Second, means of tranquilizing and invigorating exercise, as in good quiet roads and walks. . . . Third, extended landscapes, to refresh and delight the eye."[18] This first fully evolved urban park was to be an artful retreat for city dwellers, poorer and richer, who endured crowded living conditions, treeless streets laid out in gridiron fashion, loud noise, unpleasant odors, traffic chaos, limited sunlight, and unclean air. One of the New Yorkers who sought recreation there was Vaux himself. "I saw Mr. Vaux skating around the lake," wrote H. Van Buren Magonigle in the winter of 1881. At the time, the future architect was a young assistant in Vaux's office. That moon-cold night he remembered seeing his kindly mentor "with his hands behind him and his eyes on the ice, perhaps thinking of how he had helped to make the lake and establish those shores."[19]

"Rustic summer house (Kinderberg)," n.d. NYPL Digital Collections.

Vaux, more than his better-known collaborator, found himself often in the unenviable position of advocating for the preservation of his and Olmsted's masterpiece. Vaux's contemporaries recognized and honored him for his unflagging guardianship of the park ideal. "To Calvert Vaux more than to any other man New York city owes a debt of gratitude for the fact that Central Park, in spite of attacks on every side, has been held secure against harmful invasion, and has been developed strictly on the lines of its original conception," states a brief biography written shortly after his death.[20] Vaux's cherished brother-in-law, Jervis McEntee, had closely followed the park's development since providing paintings of its future appearance for the Greensward competition entry. "It is a magnificent pleasure ground," McEntee confided to his diary in May 1886, "and will always remain a monument to its designers, Vaux and Olmsted, and to Vaux's faithfulness and persistence in defending and protecting it at crucial periods in its management."[21]

Central Park represented the largest public construction project undertaken by an American city. "Truly," noted William Robinson, the renowned Irish gardener who spurred the wild gardening movement, "the transformation of a tract of swamp and rocks into one of the most beautiful parks in the world is a striking monument of American skill and perseverance."[22] Of the many accolades that Central Park received in Vaux's lifetime, the words of the art critic Clarence Cook, who had known Vaux from his earliest days in America, must have been among the most heartening. Speaking of the partnership of Olmsted and Vaux, Cook reflected: "It would hardly have been possible to find in our community two men better fitted by education, by experience, and by combination of valuable qualities, to carry out so difficult an undertaking as that of Central Park."[23] Although his authorship was contested during his lifetime and later overlooked, Vaux, supported by allies in politics and the press, resolutely defended the design created in his home during the autumn and winter of 1857–58.

"Lower End of Mall, Central Park," 1901, photochrome print. Library of Congress Prints and Photographs Division.

View of Hillside. Photo by JoEllen Hundeland.

Hillside Cemetery, Middletown, NY

(1860)

One of the first projects to come to Olmsted and Vaux after their selection as designers of Central Park was for a rural cemetery in Middletown, New York, about twenty-five miles west of Newburgh. A center of the regional economy, the young city owed its prosperity and development primarily to one man, attorney James E. Pronk. When he had first come to Middletown in 1849, Pronk found it a small village "feeling the quickening pulses of a new life" with the recent construction of the Erie Railroad.[1] As president of the village, he advanced street improvements, promoted the construction of hotels, instituted a fire department, opened a lyceum that housed a public library, and took action to bring additional rail lines to town.

But of all his many accomplishments Pronk's fellow citizens recognized that his "best and greatest gift" to Middletown was beautiful Hillside Cemetery: "We owe to him its conception, its organization, its maintenance, its beauties."[2] In 1860, Pronk organized a nondenominational cemetery association, serving as its first president. After they acquired forty-four acres of undeveloped elevated land just west of the town center, Pronk took the lead in securing the services of a landscape designer. Following his "advice and influence," remembered a contemporary, "Vaux and Olmsted, the best landscape gardeners in the country," were hired to transform the property into a new rural cemetery.[3] A local newspaper reported that the project would be planned and supervised by Vaux, and it is clear from cemetery records and diary entries of Alfred J. Bloor, who assisted the partners during these years, that Vaux took primary responsibility for the undertaking.[4]

The earliest rural cemetery of significance in the United States was Mount Auburn

Map of Middletown (detail), 1903. From A. H. Muller, *Atlas of Orange County, New York*.

in Boston, which opened in 1831. Its winding carriage ways and leafy setting became a model for other forest and lawn burial grounds. After 1847, when New York State passed the Rural Cemetery Act, such large nondenominational places of interment, which were maintained as nonprofit businesses, became increasingly common. Vaux would have been familiar with the philosophy and design of rural cemeteries from his days with Downing, who had served as "Rural Architect" of Evergreens Cemetery in Brooklyn. The "variety of woodland, and lawn," one newspaper reported, "the winding avenues, . . . [and] the lakes" were some of the "striking features of the place."[5] These elements would recur in Vaux's plan for the Middletown cemetery.

Most of the construction of the cemetery was done during the summer of 1860. Early the following spring, two thousand shade trees were planted along the edges of its two miles of roadways. The grounds were consecrated in May, and in July the first interment took place. Before long, families of soldiers who had fallen in the early days of the Civil War would lay claim to numerous gravesites.

Vaux's 1860 plan for Hillside was preserved in a map drawn by Otis Chickering, an engineer associate of the firm.[6] There were to be 2,500 lots, three hundred feet square, with a special section reserved for indigent burials. The layout took full advantage of the prominent site, and a casual observer might have noticed some similarities to the plan of Central Park. An entrance in the northeast corner of the grounds led to a circuit drive that skirted the low-lying terrain and two manmade lakes. Other serpentine roads diverged toward the interior of the cemetery. In the hilly midsection, a Ramble-like network of roads and footpaths prevailed. Carriage and walkways eventually led to Observatory Hill, the highest point of the landscape, where visitors could enjoy a fine view of the town and surrounding countryside.

To enhance this experience, Vaux proposed a forty-foot-tall masonry observation tower. Such a feature had been introduced at Mount Auburn where, from its medieval-style stone turret, the art historian Kerry Dean Carso has noted, "one can continue in a melancholy vein on the fleeting nature of life, a reverie encouraged by

View of Hillside. Photo by JoEllen Hundeland.

Vaux, "Design for a Tower for Hillside Cemetery." From *Villas and Cottages* (1864).

the views of sentimental monuments to the dead visible in the landscape below."[7] In repeating the architectural form, Vaux and the cemetery directors must certainly have sought to evoke the same feeling. Vaux's tower, however, was more up-to-date in style, taking its cue from his friend Jacob Wrey Mould's Italian Gothic design for the campanile of All Souls Unitarian Church in New York. But neither Mould's nor Vaux's towers were ever built.

Vaux intended Hillside Cemetery, like other rural burial grounds, to be a place of reflection. It was an emotive woodland landscape that expressed the Transcendentalist faith in the spiritual power of nature to comfort and heal. Vaux would surely have agreed with the late Swiss landscape architect Dieter Kienast, designer of the Fürstenwald Cemetery at Chur, in his belief in the comforting power of landscape: "Gradually, thoughts of the dead mingle with our experience of the immediacy of landscape and nature."[8]

View of Hillside. Photo by JoEllen Hundeland.

Long Meadow, Prospect Park. Photo © Matthew X. Kiernan/New York Big Apple Images.

Prospect Park, Brooklyn

(1865; with F. L. Olmsted)

In 1903, shortly after the death of Olmsted (Vaux had died eight years earlier), Alfred Janson Bloor, a close associate of both men in the 1860s, told the readers of the *New-York Tribune* that "as for the Brooklyn park, I have this to say for the very first time . . . in public: My conviction on personal and in some degree on exclusive knowledge is that Calvert Vaux, the pupil, as regards landscape and ground decorative effects, of A. J. Downing, was the sole designer of the guiding lines and main features of Prospect Park, and that his share in those, and, indeed, in every detail of the Central Park was at least equal to that of Olmsted." Bloor shared with the *Tribune*'s readers his "exclusive knowledge" of the genesis of Prospect Park:

> On the outbreak of the Civil War, Mr. Olmsted, being appointed general secretary of the United States Sanitary Commission, asked me, as did the Rev. Dr. Bellows, its president, to quit serving the Central Park and help them as resident Washington secretary in their work for the organization. . . . I did so, but at the war's close I rejoined forces with Vaux, who had throughout remained at his professional post in New-York, whereas Olmsted—some time in 1863, I don't recall the exact date—resigned from the Sanitary Commission and was placed in charge of the great Mariposa estate in California, where he remained till some time after peace returned.
>
> When, the war at an end, I got back to New-York, Mr. Vaux confided to me that he had just come to an understanding with J. S. T. Stranahan—"the first citizen of Brooklyn," to give him the title later ascribed

"Prospect Park View from the Reservoir Looking West," 1860. From *Annual Reports of the Brooklyn Park Commissioners, 1861–1873.* NYPL Digital Collections.

> to him—as to the designs for that then separate city of a park on similar ample and artistic lines to those of the Central Park; but owing to certain of those political and personal complications which so often interfere with and sometimes wholly prevent operations of public utility and wide scope, the preliminary work of design would have to be done in secrecy. He therefore asked me to reopen my office in the same building with his own, so that I might be in easy call for possibly needed assistance, without the intervention in his own office of parties more given to irresponsible gossip than to professional reticence. . . . I complied with Mr. Vaux's request, and the main lines of Prospect Park, as they now exist, were, I am safe in saying, mostly designed in my office—sometimes by very late gaslight—by none other than Calvert Vaux.[1]

Prospect Park was the brainchild of James S. T. Stranahan, a self-made man of wealth who undertook a mission to improve the cultural standing of his hometown. "The fact that Brooklyn was considered an intellectual wasteland by New Yorkers, who even regarded its citizens as lesser beings," the historian David P. Colley has observed, "inspired Stranahan to enrich his city through the advancement of the arts. . . . But it was his vision of public space to rival Central Park that was his most fervent endeavor."[2] In 1864, as president of the city's park commission, he turned to Vaux for advice, but only after the commissioners had, in 1861, engaged the military engineer Egbert Viele to prepare a park plan. Vaux found himself in an awkward position reminiscent of the earliest days of Central Park, when he had striven to have Viele's initial design overturned. Vaux had even been forced to fend off a lawsuit by the embittered engineer. It all was a thorn in his memory. This must have been the reason for the secrecy to which Bloor referred surrounding Vaux's early work on the Brooklyn project.

In February 1865, Vaux quietly expressed to Stranahan his negative opinion of Viele's Brooklyn park scheme. Once again, Vaux perceived how Viele had terribly missed the point of what was before him: he had staked out his design around an existing reservoir on land that was bisected by Flatbush Avenue, a major city thoroughfare. Vaux's correction was simple but radical: to create a truly grand park the split had to be repaired and areas beyond the current boundaries acquired. In the words of Olmsted scholar Charles Beveridge, while Olmsted was out West, Vaux proposed "to move the entire Prospect Park site to the west of Flatbush Avenue and expand its area to include what became the Long Meadow and Prospect Lake. The oval area for the plaza at the northern entrance of the park was also included in this

"Sheep in Prospect Park," 1900–1905. Library of Congress Prints and Photographs Division.

expansion."[3] Vaux had worked a change that was momentous for the future success of the park.

Conceptualizing was one thing, executing was another. Vaux believed that to move forward with the Brooklyn project he needed his old friend at his side. Eventually, he succeeded in persuading Olmsted to resign his post with the Mariposa mining estate. Olmsted arrived back in New York from California in November 1865 and promptly resumed his partnership with Vaux. On January 24, 1866, they presented their preliminary report to Stranahan and the park commissioners. A few days later, the *Brooklyn Daily Union* told its readers that a topographical survey had been conducted and that Olmsted and Vaux had presented a general layout along with an extensive written report. Their plan incorporated Vaux's earlier suggestion that the original boundaries be significantly modified to improve the overall character of the park. With all the information before them, the commissioners could see that such modifications were required. Moreover, they were confident that although the proposed changes involved a considerable enlargement of the grounds, their constituents would appreciate that the increased space and highly picturesque views thus

Olmsted, Vaux & Co., *Design for Prospect Park*, 1871. Courtesy Prospect Park Archives.

secured would far outweigh the expense involved in acquiring the acreage. Hence, they deemed the modifications "justifiable on economical principles."[4]

Such a sweeping step, however, would necessitate the public's assent. Within a week the *Union* informed its readers that the park commissioners were "now prepared to present to the people of the city, a plan for the park which they feel justly confident will win the confidence and hearty acquiesce of all." Without mentioning Viele, the paper announced that the commissioners had engaged new designers, "the most distinguished and the most competent landscape-gardeners in the country." The article went on to enumerate the natural benefits of the revised site. Undoubtedly recounting testimony heard from Vaux, the newspaper emphasized how superior it was to the land barren of "natural advantages" that Olmsted and Vaux had confronted at Central Park.

> Here they will have much more varied opportunities to produce landscape effects. Forest trees of good growth and stately proportion; hills affording not only prominent points of attraction in the immediate view of the park, but also of themselves affording wide and beautiful views of the ocean and the level land stretching southward to the sea; water bottom on which can be formed lakes of over a mile in length and of proportionate width; wide reaches of meadow . . . ; groves where the multitudes of wild vines and flowers which cluster about the winding paths can be indefinitely multiplied and extended. . . . We may rest assured that if without them, Messrs Olmsted and Vaux were enabled to make of Central Park the miniature Paradise which it is, with them they will make Prospect Park proportionately more attractive and more powerful in its elevating influences.[5]

On March 20, 1866, the *Union* followed up its earlier favorable notice with a long article devoted to the substance of the report, explaining to its readers, in language "not quite so formal and technical as that of Messrs Vaux & Co.," the importance of adopting the new borders. "The first thing called for is a change in the boundaries of the park," the editors explained, "to be commenced by abandoning all that portion lying east of Flatbush Avenue." As Vaux had already suggested, the partners proposed that this steep land, which held a reservoir, be exchanged for other, more open property. In this way, the new park could better fulfill its goal of offering visitors a far-reaching pastoral landscape. "The first thing and essential thing to be demanded in a large park is a sense of enlarged freedom," proclaimed the paper, parroting the

"Prospect Park, Brooklyn," 1897. Library of Congress Prints and Photographs Division.

landscape architects. "People go there to get rid of narrow streets, the buildings shutting out the skies, the hard, rough pavements driving away the grass, the limitations to the eye which stand on every side. They go to get liberty to breathe fresh air, to see a variety of pleasant things, to have the vision expanded and tempted to stretches of beautiful scenery, and to have contact with nature in its simplicity and beauty."[6] It would be achieved with consummate skill and unmatched results in their plans for Prospect Park, which were approved later that year.

If Vaux, as the initiator of this engaging program, could give us a tour of the 526-acre Prospect Park landscape, he would surely first call special attention to the Long Meadow. Created by draining swampy meadowland, the gently rolling greensward stretches nearly a mile along the northwestern border of the park inviting leisurely activity as visitors enter the park. He would also highlight the Ravine, a 150-acre picturesque woodland in the heart of the park, kindred with the 38-acre Ramble in Central Park. The woodland is traversed by the man-made waterway that meanders through the park over constructed cascades and into a series of pools, each creating a different type of landscape, before opening into the sixty-acre artificial Prospect Park Lake. With its irregular wooded shoreline shaped with coves and peninsulas and its wooded islands, the lake evokes a feeling of mystery at the southern end of the park. Other attractions Vaux would point out are the Concert Grove, where visitors enjoyed open-air concerts played by an orchestra installed offshore on an islet in the lake; the popular Children's Pool, a small pond in the northeast section of the park called the Vale, where young parkgoers would sail miniature toy boats; and the Nethermead, a gentle meadow offering quiet experience of nature near the center of the park. Vaux would certainly take us up Lookout Hill, the highest point in the park, to see the commanding views of New York Harbor, the Atlantic Ocean, and the hills of New Jersey—the prospect that gave the park its name.

Vaux and Olmsted's plan also included the Plaza (today Grand Army Plaza) at the main entrance to the park. Originally a single jet fountain, the Fountain of the Golden Spray, was installed in the center of the spacious oval public square, but in 1873, Vaux's Plaza Fountain replaced it with a fantastic centerpiece that drew

"A Glimpse of Lake, Prospect Park," 1905–1915. Library of Congress Prints and Photographs Division.

inspiration from the circular seventeenth-century Latona Fountain and Basin at Versailles. An exceptional example of High Victorian art (it rivaled for attention Jacob Wrey Mould's City Hall Park Fountain in Manhattan), the immense fountain resembled a half-submerged dome, consisting of "two tiers of radial pieces, of an ornamental design, weighing between two and three tons a piece," the *Brooklyn Daily Eagle* reported.[7] For the molded tiers, Vaux used a new material, *béton-coignet,* recently developed in France and replacing far more expensive granite and marble in construction. Water poured down in a multitude of rivulets from a crownlike feature into a wide circular basin. Many jets and sprays joined in the aquatic festivities. Beguiled by the possibilities for nighttime light displays that municipal gas made possible, Vaux designed arched openings ringing the bases of both tiers which held colored glass panes. At night, internal gaslights set the stained-glass windows aglow, creating a vibrant spectacle. Extravagant resources were needed to activate

Concert Grove, c. 1910. Courtesy Prospect Park Archives/Bob Levine Collection.

"The Fountain in the Plaza," 1860?. NYPL Digital Collections.

this extravagant conception: the fountain consumed more than fifty thousand gallons of water per hour. For many years, Brooklyn's illuminated marvel attracted evening visitors from all parts of town. "Nothing could excel it," proclaimed a voice in the local press, "short of absolutely and unmistakably unclouded moonshine."[8]

As he had done at Central Park, Vaux contributed important structures to the Prospect Park landscape. In Brooklyn, however, the prepossessing natural terrain received fewer architectural embellishments than the earlier park. But like those in Central Park, the features that Vaux planned in Brooklyn both filled a specific requirement and synchronized with the bucolic scenery. The Meadowport Arch (1868) and Endale Arch (1867), for example, support carriage drives along their upper levels and provide pedestrians safe passage below. Moreover, for those coming into the grounds from outside the park, the vaulted spaces function as vestibules to the world of nature they are about to enter. The arches focus the pedestrian's attention on what lies ahead, framing an alluring picture of the Long Meadow. Exiting these tunnel-like spaces, walkers might immediately feel a sense of "enlarged freedom" evoked by the sweeping green.

Other instances of framing scenery occur within the park. One bright spring afternoon in 1874, a newspaper reporter saw James Stranahan standing at one end of the Cleft Ridge Span directing the attention of two women companions "to a feature which, when taken in by others, furnished one of the nicest pieces of landscape to be seen in the Park." Looking in this direction, the observer continued, "one takes in a portion of the multitude at the music stand—just enough to fringe the picture; immediately beyond the arch is the lawn, where are little parties of young folks playing croquet, others lounging listlessly on the grass, and away beyond a vista of trees, until the perspective is made abrupt by the hill. It was indeed no inept picture that Mr. Stranahan selected from that standpoint."[9] The enduring association of the longtime president of the park board with Calvert Vaux had accustomed him to the landscape architect's way of seeing.

Other structures Vaux added to the landscape addressed the physical comfort of park visitors. The Cleft Ridge Span and other masonry arches kept both carriage traffic and riders on horseback separate from pedestrians as they strolled the entwining network of pathways that Vaux and Olmsted threaded through the park grounds. Rustic wooden bridges eased visitors' passage through the Ravine and enhanced its picturesque atmosphere. Throughout the park, rustic seats, covered and open, invited

Endale Arch, c. 1890. Courtesy Prospect Park Archives/Bob Levine Collection.

"Looking west from under Cleft Ridge Span," 1871–1881. Library of Congress Prints and Photographs Division.

visitors to sit and enjoy the scenery. A number of buildings displayed styles popular at the time. These included vernacular imitations such as the quaint Thatched Cottage (1867; destroyed by fire in 1937) and the homely stone Dairy (1869; demolished). The most architecturally defined area of the park is the Concert Grove, where low walls embraced audiences while they attended musical performances. Surfaces were enlivened with floral relief carvings by Thomas Wisedell, an up-and-coming British architect Vaux had invited to come to America in 1868 when he visited England. The keynote structure is the Concert Grove Pavilion (1874; restored in 2021). The billowing roof and supporting cast iron columns of the open-air shelter are a colorful

"Oak Bridge," n.d. NYPL Digital Collections.

"Rustic Arbor," n.d. NYPL Digital Collections.

visual feast. The final contribution that Vaux made to the Prospect Park landscape is the 1889 carriage and pedestrian Terrace Bridge. The graceful metal span joins the Concert Grove with Lookout Hill and the Peninsula.

Vaux also made ambitious designs for structures that were never built. Perhaps they fell victim to the economic slump that followed the Panic of 1873. For the Concert Grove, he proposed (c. 1871) an extraordinary trough where horses might quench their thirst. While they did, they and their carriage passengers and mounts would have enjoyed shelter from the elements beneath a huge round canopy that rested on a single slender support, a fanciful structure that looked like a gigantic child's spinning top. Vaux's largest unrealized project for Prospect Park was an immense brick tower to be erected on Lookout Hill (1873). Surmounted by an elaborate wooden porch, it far exceeded in magnificence and height his earlier design for the observatory intended for similar circumstances at Middletown's Hillside Cemetery. Looking at his perspective drawing, one can only imagine what it would have been like to survey the park and the world around it from that midair perch.

If, in the early 1870s, Calvert Vaux had taken a stroll along the newly created paths of Prospect Park, he might have paused to reflect on the impact of the concept he introduced to his Brooklyn clients in 1865. Around him would have been

Thatched Cottage. From *1885 Annual Report to the Brooklyn Park Commissioners.* Courtesy Prospect Park Archives.

Vaux, *Design for Observatory to Be Erected on Look-Out Hill.* Courtesy Prospect Park Archives/Bob Levine Collection.

Vaux, *Shelter Proposed to Be Erected on the Carriage Concourse.* Courtesy Prospect Park Archives.

"Prospect Park, Brooklyn." From *Picturesque America,* vol. 2 (1874).

Trees at sunrise in Prospect Park. Photo by ProspectParkEnjoyer/Wikimedia.

a landscape of about five hundred and fifty acres he had carefully crafted. With the help of his brilliant partner, the park had come into being. Vaux would have appreciated seeing people enjoying the grounds, even in that early stage, knowing it would take more years for the trees and plantings to mature as he had envisioned. Meanwhile, hundreds of ordinary people were experiencing a landscape he had designed for their pleasure and relaxation. His was a place where humanity and nature could coexist, a Claude-glass world exempt from the bullying progress of manifest destiny.

Vaux might also have reflected on how both the Brooklyn and Manhattan parks had validated his belief that landscape architecture was, first and foremost, an art. Perhaps nothing would have pleased him more than seeing fellow artists and writers using his and Olmsted's designs as subjects for their own creations. His friend William Cullen Bryant had recently honored both Prospect Park and

Central Park in his iconic book *Picturesque America; or, The Land We Live In,* praising them as marvels of the continent.[10] Vaux would have been delighted to see James Douglas Woodward's newly minted collage of Prospect Park scenes, just as others had paid tribute to Central Park. In Vaux's lifetime, many artists, including William Merritt Chase, T. A. Richards, and anonymous amateurs, would choose the new parks as subjects for their art. In the twentieth century, the list of those inspired by Vaux and Olmsted's works would grow even longer, especially with the addition of photographers.

A century after its creation, Prospect Park experienced a period of municipal neglect. The forlorn situation eventually attracted the attention of latter-day park advocates. Realizing what a treasure it was to Brooklyn, they formed the Prospect Park Alliance in 1987. Through their valiant efforts over the ensuing decades, the undervalued urban amenity was restored to the social, economic, and aesthetic community asset that Stranahan, Vaux, and Olmsted had imagined. Currently, the Prospect Park Alliance manages the park in partnership with the City of New York Department of Parks and Recreation. The park is listed in the National Register of Historic Places and designated a scenic landmark by the New York City Landmarks Preservation Commission.

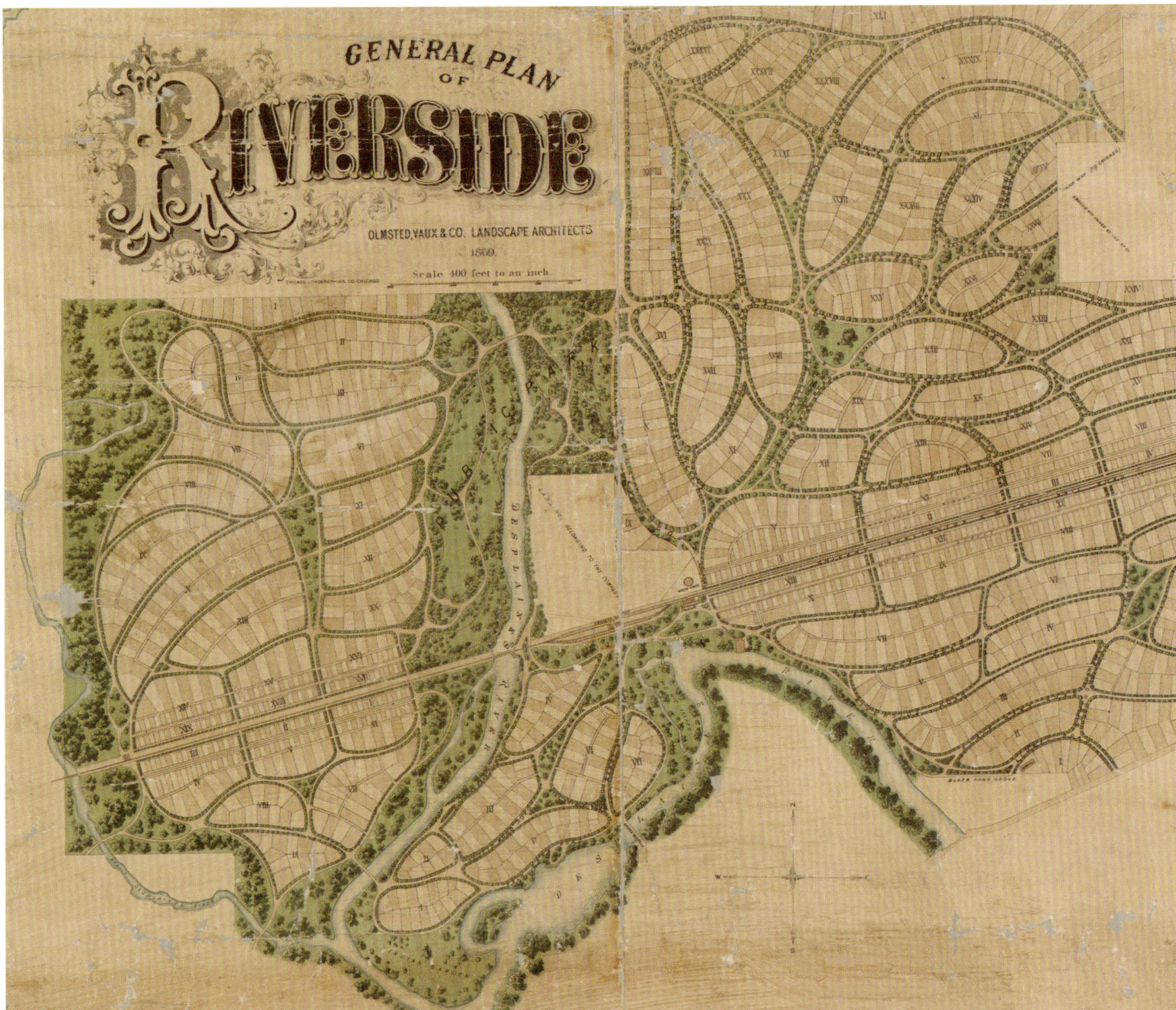

Olmsted, Vaux & Co., *General Plan of Riverside*, 1869. Courtesy Olmsted Society of Riverside.

Riverside, IL

(1868; with F. L. Olmsted)

In the spring of 1868, the Brooklyn financier Emery E. Childs conceived of creating a large, middle-class residential suburb near the growing city of Chicago. Childs soon purchased 1,600 acres of farmland twelve miles southwest of the city along the Des Plaines River. The area, which included an ancient Indigenous trail and ford, had been known since pioneer days as Riverside because of the easy access it provided for drovers to water cattle. Now the land was largely cultivated to raise vegetables for the Chicago market. Childs and his investors, forming the Riverside Improvement Company, aimed to capitalize on the increasing market for middle-class housing at a distance from the city. It would be the first large, comprehensively planned residential suburb in the country. "Those who are familiar with Morrisania, East New York, and Bergen Hill," reported the *Chicago Evening Post,* "do not need to be told how suburbs grow with us—cheap, white, a wooden house here, a grocery store there and an Irishman and his shanty and his pig between them." Riverside, which was one of several major projects Olmsted and Vaux had in hand at Chicago, would "escape this stage—the horrid stage of adolescence."[1]

In early August 1868, while Vaux was in England and Europe touring public parks and gardens and the new London Underground, Olmsted visited the site and submitted a report to the Improvement Company the following month. Although Vaux had no hand in framing it, we can assume that Vaux would have endorsed the conceptual framework that Olmsted delineated in his report, which bore both their names. The firm's reports, which often included discussion of the theory and practice of landscape architecture and urban design as well as detailed explanations of the specific plans, were typically collaborative efforts and reflected the shared vision of both men. The preliminary proposals for Riverside (and Buffalo, which Olmsted visited on his way to and from Riverside), however, were initiated by Olmsted.

Observing that Chicago had "no true suburbs or quarters in which urban and rural advantages are agreeably combined with any prospect of long continuance," Olmsted recognized the unique potential of the Riverside site. Here the river was the chief natural feature, and its banks should be preserved for public recreation. Throughout the community, beauty and utility would be combined. "Turf and trees should abound," asserted the partners. In addition, sidewalks should provide safe and pleasant passage for pedestrians, and lots should be spacious enough to accommodate individual dwellings set back from the street with ample room for gardens. Sanitation would include sewer lines, and earth closets—which Vaux had described in *Villas and Cottages*—would also be required; outhouses would be prohibited.[2] A grand boulevard would connect Riverside to Chicago, supplementing the existing rail line and adding a long linear park to the area's green assets. (The parkway was never constructed.)

Scene with lamplighter. Courtesy Riverside Historical Museum.

Returning to America in November 1868, Vaux joined Olmsted in preparing the Riverside plan. The map published in 1869 showed the land divided into eastern and western sections. Gracefully curving residential streets defined lozenge-shaped blocks. About one-fifth of the land was to be reserved as parkland for all residents. The oxbow of the Des Plaines River, which flowed along the southern boundary and through the heart of the community, would be bordered by greenspace, with a large area near the center designated as "Public Park." Other spots were designated "Picnic Grove" and "Indian Gardens" (evidence remained of the Potawatomi, the tribe that had earlier inhabited the land). A network of serpentine pedestrian paths, separated from the drives, invited residents to stroll safely through their community, crossing the river at bridges located near the northern and southern edges. The originally treeless landscape was to be filled with verdant plantings; homeowners were even required to plant a certain number of trees on their property.

Vaux and Olmsted found models for the Riverside design in Joseph Paxton's Edensor, Derbyshire, of 1842, a village of houses in many styles set in picturesque surroundings, and his Prince's Park, Liverpool of 1841. At Prince's Park, the historian Kate Colquhoun has noted, the gardener-architect introduced the "principle of exclusive housing built around the edges of the park on individual plots sold for profit."[3] Olmsted was particularly impressed by Paxton's Birkenhead Park in Liverpool, which he had visited during his tour of England in 1850. There public parkland bounded by a carriage drive was edged by stylish residences incorporated into the design.

Construction progressed rapidly. In a letter dated December 1, 1868, written by Vaux, the partners stated that they had revisited the site and "prepared plans for laying out part of the ground, ha[d] arranged contracts for grading three miles of roadways and ha[d] obtained definite estimates or tenders of contract for some of the more important items of construction."[4] The following spring, a local paper reported that several miles of roads were ready for use and a number of houses near completion for "some of our most prominent citizens." (Both Vaux and Frederick Withers received commissions from Riverside clients.) In general, the place already presented "a most attractive appearance."[5]

On May 8, 1869, Vaux and Olmsted were on hand to conduct a tour of the rising development. The 1869 *General Plan of Riverside* bearing the firm name Olmsted, Vaux & Company, Landscape Architects, was likely printed for the occasion. Five hundred people boarded ten of the Pullman Company's most elegant dining cars to make the journey from the city to the Riverside station, where some fifty carriages

View south from School House. Courtesy Riverside Historical Museum.

awaited to drive them around the property. Olmsted and Vaux guided this "novel caravan," pointing out the salient features of "river, woods and highlands." Later, the party heard Olmsted give a brief address. Acting the part of sales agent for the Improvement Company, he touted Riverside as possessing "superior advantages over any park ever laid out in the United States." The former farmland, he said, was very fertile and pleasantly elevated above the surrounding prairie. Moreover, the Des Plaines River "was unsurpassed for its general beauty." In full booster mode, Olmsted proclaimed to the assembled crowd that there was no reason why Riverside "should not be made the most attractive place on the continent." For good measure, he assured this audience of prospective buyers that the company was an exemplary one with which to do business.[6]

This last boast soon proved to be hollow. Taken in by Childs's predictions of imminent fortune, Olmsted and Vaux had agreed to payment in property rather than the five dollars per acre they originally had proposed. Childs, however, had greatly inflated the value of the lots they were given, and by June 1869, warning signs were apparent. Vaux told Olmsted he thought "the Company looks a rather kite flying affair." Moreover, Childs had decided to appropriate land reserved for the public park for his own mansion. Vaux wrote Olmsted, who was then at Riverside, that he "objected utterly, wholly and without qualification" to this disregard of "the keynote of the whole design." He declared that he "would be no party to it," admonished Olmsted that "I trust you will present our resignation without fail if this preposterous arrangement is preserved in."[7] By the fall of 1870, the partners had severed all ties with the company. The directors, however, eventually laid out the eastern thousand acres of Riverside according to the Olmsted and Vaux plan, which was promoted in their June 1871 brochure. Most of the section planned for west of the river was not implemented.

At Riverside, Olmsted and Vaux created a fully evolved example of the modern notions of home life that had been fostered in America by Andrew Jackson Downing. By uniting tranquil natural surroundings, communal recreational activities, and easy access to town with comprehensive planning and civil engineering, they defined a community that combined urban and rural advantages. In 1969 the Department of the Interior designated Riverside a National Historic Landmark.

Gates Circle and Chapin Parkway. Photo by Andy Olenick.

Buffalo Parks and Parkway System

(1868–1870; with F. L. Olmsted)

In the years immediately after the Civil War, Buffalo emerged as vibrant hub of activity. A growing city situated on the eastern shore of Lake Erie, Buffalo commanded a strategic position, serving as the gateway to the navigable waters of the four westernmost Great Lakes and making it a pivotal player in the bustling Midwest grain trade. Wheat carried here by steamer was stored in newly invented grain elevators until it was shipped east to New York, by way of the Erie Canal or the burgeoning railroads.

Progressive-minded civic leaders wished to seize the moment of great prosperity to realize the promise of Joseph Ellicott's forward-looking 1804 city plan and transform Buffalo into a true metropolis. In the spring of 1868, William Dorsheimer, a prominent attorney, invited Olmsted to advise on the creation of a large country park, like New York City's Central Park, which Dorsheimer greatly admired. That August, while Vaux was on a tour of England and Europe that would keep him away until November, Olmsted traveled to Buffalo and, after looking over the city and its environs, was invited to address a public meeting. His remarks that evening were a historic moment in the history of the nascent American park movement.[1]

Rather than advocating for one large park like Central or Prospect Park, Olmsted proposed that the city invest in three separate parks, each tailored to different forms of recreation. The largest of these, The Park (the city changed the name to Delaware Park in the 1890s), three miles north of downtown, would be designed as a country park, easing the mind for receptivity to nature. Its 350 acres comprised

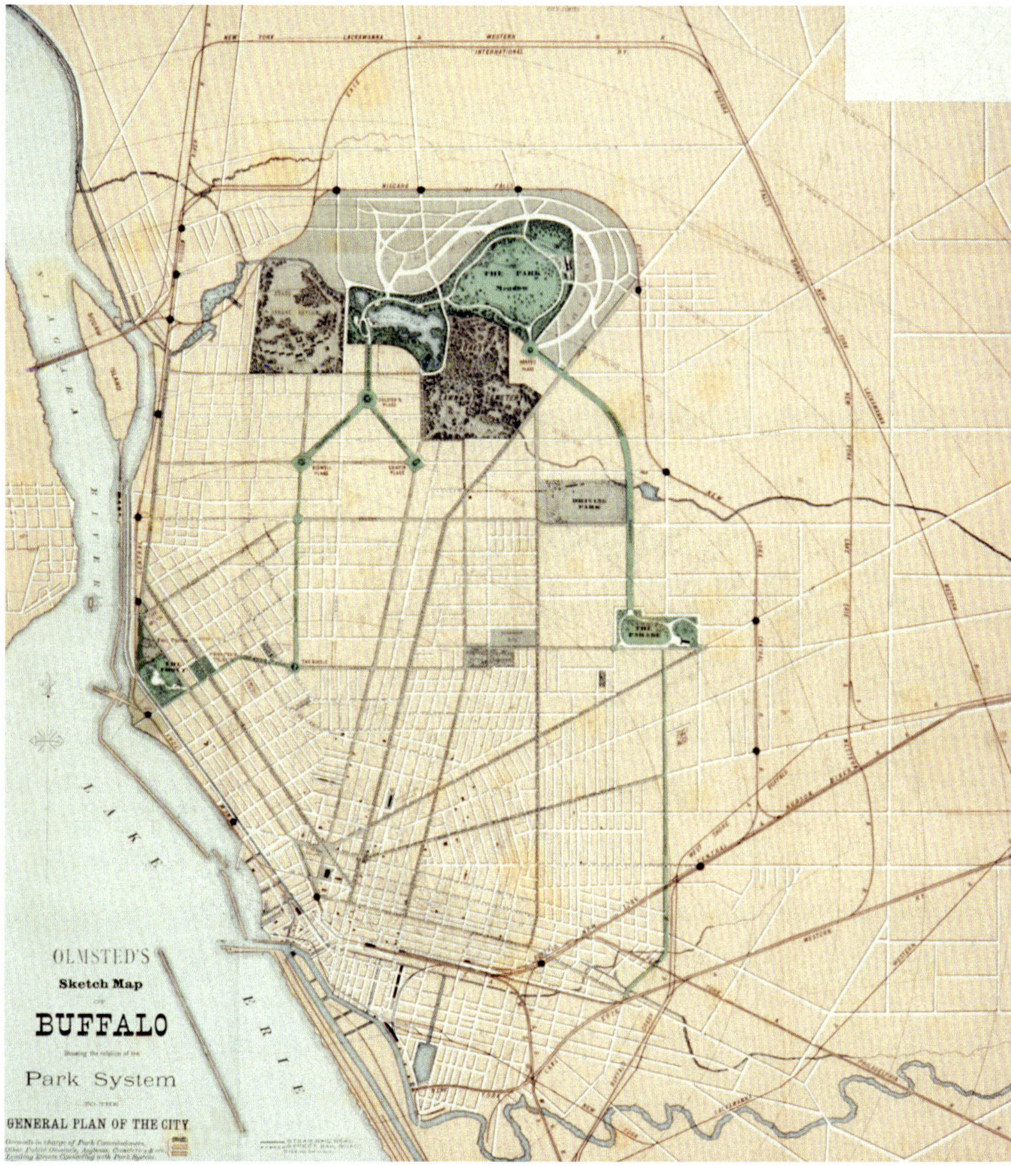

Olmsted's Sketch Map of Buffalo, 1881. Author's collection.

a large meadow reminiscent of Prospect Park's Long Meadow, a picturesque lake formed by damming a stream that meandered through the site, and woodland areas. The Front, located on a thirty-five-acre site on the western border of the city, overlooked the spot where the Niagara River leaves Lake Erie on its way to Niagara Falls. An expansive terrace would offer panoramic vistas of the lake and river, all the way to the distant Canadian shore, and a place to watch the sun set over the water.

A field for active sports would complement but not compete with the aim of scenic preservation. The fifty-acre Parade (today Martin Luther King Jr. Park) was located on the east side of the city. Featuring a large sports field where, as its name implied, military drills could be performed, The Parade would also have a grand eatery and dance hall, a place of merry assembly.

Olmsted went on to explain that these three parks would be interconnected

South bank of lake from north bank, 1872. From *Annual Report of the Buffalo Park Commissioners* (1873).

The Parade, watercolor commissioned for 1876 Centennial Exhibition. Courtesy Buffalo History Museum.

by a series of wide residential boulevards, which he and Vaux termed "parkways." They had first introduced the concept in their 1867 report to the Prospect Park commissioners, where they described two-hundred-foot-wide thoroughfares lined with multiple rows of elm trees and divided into separate ways for vehicles, equestrians, and pedestrians. The Eastern Parkway, begun in 1870, stretched from Grand Army Plaza to the eastern border of Brooklyn, extending the park experience into the farther reaches of the city's residential district. The Buffalo parkways, in addition to being elegant residential thoroughfares like Paris's famous Avenue de l'Impératrice, would serve as linear parks to the neighborhoods they traversed. It is possible that the introduction of circles where major parkways met was Vaux's suggestion, inspired by his recent visit to Paris, where such roundabouts were a major feature.

In August 1869, Olmsted and Vaux traveled to Buffalo to explain their fully developed plan. (It was during this visit that Olmsted gathered a group at Niagara Falls to propose that the state acquire the land around the famous Cataract for a park.) City officials soon approved Olmsted and Vaux's far-ranging proposal, which they recognized would define the development of the city's nonindustrial areas. In 1870 the firm's engineer associate George K. Radford took up residence to supervise construction. William McMillan, a Scottish gardener employed at Prospect Park, was hired at Olmsted's recommendation to oversee the planting phase.

Entrance to the Front, 1890s. Courtesy James Mendola.

Lincoln Parkway, c. 1900. Author's collection.

Cyclist in Delaware Park, c. 1890. Courtesy Janice and Dale Rossi.

Lincoln Parkway Bridge, 1872. From *Annual Report of the Buffalo Park Commissioners* (1873).

Delaware Street viaduct, c. 1890. Courtesy James Mendola.

Gala Water from the west landing, Spire Head in distance, 1885. Photo by A. W. Simon. Courtesy Janice and Dale Rossi.

By 1874, Buffalo had become the first American city to possess a fully realized park and parkway system.

Like Central and Prospect Parks, the Buffalo park system was a collaborative effort, although here too Vaux designed important park structures. These included the Boat House and the Moorish-inspired polygonal Spire Head summerhouse in The Park. Even more exotic was the extravagant Parade House, a multicolored masterpiece of turned and carved wood. The fusion of restaurant, dance hall, and theater was particularly popular with the many German families who lived in the neighborhood and who frequented it especially on Sunday when beer was served there but nowhere else in town. The Parade House, surely the most elaborate and festive architecture ever to grace an American park landscape, was a monument to democratic camaraderie—a goal Olmsted and Vaux hoped their parks would promote.

Boathouse, 1875. From *Annual Report of the Buffalo Park Commissioners* (1877).

Spire Head House, 1897. Photo by Webster & Allen. Courtesy Janice and Dale Rossi.

West veranda of the Parade House, 1883. Photo by George Barker. Courtesy Janice and Dale Rossi.

Delaware Park. Photo by Andy Olenick.

For many years, Buffalo neglected its national legacy of parks and urban planning. Humboldt, the grandest of the parkways, was destroyed in the 1960s to make way for the Kensington Expressway. In the 1970s, however, a small number of forward-looking citizens led the way toward restoring what remained of the park system. A preservation milestone was reached in 1982 when the extant elements of the park and parkway system earned listing in the National Register of Historic Places. The pioneering Friends of Olmsted Parks evolved into the Buffalo Olmsted Parks Conservancy. Modeled on the Central Park Conservancy, the Buffalo organization works with the city parks department to continue the long-term effort to restore Buffalo's historic urban landscapes, including advocating for the full restoration of Humboldt Parkway.

Frederic Edwin Church, *Clouds over Olana,* 1872, oil on off-white paper. Collection Olana State Historic Site, New York State Office of Parks, Recreation and Historic Preservation (NYS OPRHP).

Frederic Edwin Church House / Olana, Hudson, NY

(1870+)

When Frederic Edwin Church returned from an extended trip to the Middle East and Europe in 1869, he stood at the forefront of American art. His shimmering vision of Niagara Falls and his imposing *Heart of the Andes* had established his reputation as a painter of landscapes of extraordinary clarity, expansiveness, and Romantic emotion. Nine years earlier, Church had purchased 126 acres south of the village of Hudson, New York, where he and his new wife Isabel had built a small cottage and begun transforming the land into a working farm. In 1866 they added an eighteen-acre hilltop parcel to their land and began planning a new house. Church turned to Calvert Vaux to collaborate with him in the design of the mansion he would call Olana, in reference to a Persian hilltop treasure-storehouse. The site commanded a breathtaking view, a real-world counterpart to the far-ranging scenery Church depicted on his canvases. To the north, it extended as far as Albany; to the west, it took in the Catskill Mountains and the former home of his revered teacher, Thomas Cole; and to the south, it surveyed the great river coursing, in the words of the historian David Schuyler, "back and forth through some of the most majestic scenery in the world."[1]

Inspired by the architecture of the Middle East, Church knew what he wanted in the new house, but he relied on Vaux's architectural skill, sympathetic aesthetic philosophy, and his love for the Hudson River Valley landscape to realize his dream.[2] Vaux had already designed residences in relation to river overlooks. Fitting models were the Hoyt house at Staatsburg, Findlay house at Newburgh, the cottage that Jervis McEntee, Vaux's brother-in-law and Church's one-time student, built at Kings-

Frederic Edwin Church, *Cosy Cottage,* c. 1870–72, oil on board. Collection Olana State Historic Site, NYS OPRHP.

Frederic Edwin Church, *Apple Blossoms at Olana,* 1872, oil on academy board. Collection Olana State Historic Site, NYS OPRHP.

Arthur Parton, *Looking Southwest over Church's Farm from the Sienghenburg,* 1884, oil on canvas. Collection Olana State Historic Site.

ton. Church especially admired the Catskill mountain scenery McEntee commanded from his hilltop dwelling. ("The Hills about [McEntee's] Home," he remarked years later, ". . . seem a fitting monument to his memory.")[3] Other houses with belvedere perspectives appeared in the page of *Villas and Cottages.* Poring over plans that Vaux and he had worked out for Olana, shortly before construction began in 1870, Church exclaimed that "the picture from each window will be really marvelous."[4] Together they had fashioned Olana, flawlessly melding Church's aesthetic aspirations with Vaux's architectural genius. One evening in 1872, as construction was nearing completion, Vaux and McEntee dined with the Churches at Olana. "It is certainly a beautiful house," McEntee confided to his diary, "and commands one of the finest views of river & mountains in the country."[5]

Olana occupied a privileged site on the property, commanding a varied prospect encompassing woods, orchards, and fields, all of which provided the Church family with agricultural income. Together with this functioning farm, Church wished to harmonize the surrounding home grounds with the picturesque, exotic beauty of his hillcrest residence. Over the years, he took as much interest in devising roads and landscape features as he did in building and maintaining the house itself. It is natural to assume that the same collaborative spirit between Church and his architect characterized his relationship with Vaux the landscape architect. Vaux frequently visited Church while the house was under construction, so it is likely that he offered his advice and expertise on how the landscape might be fashioned according to Church's vision.

Clearly, the landscape of Olana echoed the country park aesthetic embodied in Central Park. Church knew well that great fictive rural landscape. Beginning in 1871, while Olana was under construction, Church served a two-year term on the park's board of commissioners, where he was an ally of Olmsted and Vaux in the defense of the Greensward plan. He would have been thoroughly familiar with the way roads and paths followed the terrain, avoiding straight lines and right angles. He may even have heard Vaux repeat his dictum that in the park, architecture was subordinate to nature, and he surely appreciated the rapport that existed between Vaux's Belvedere Castle and the greater landscape.

Throughout his property, Church sought to create an aesthetic unity among

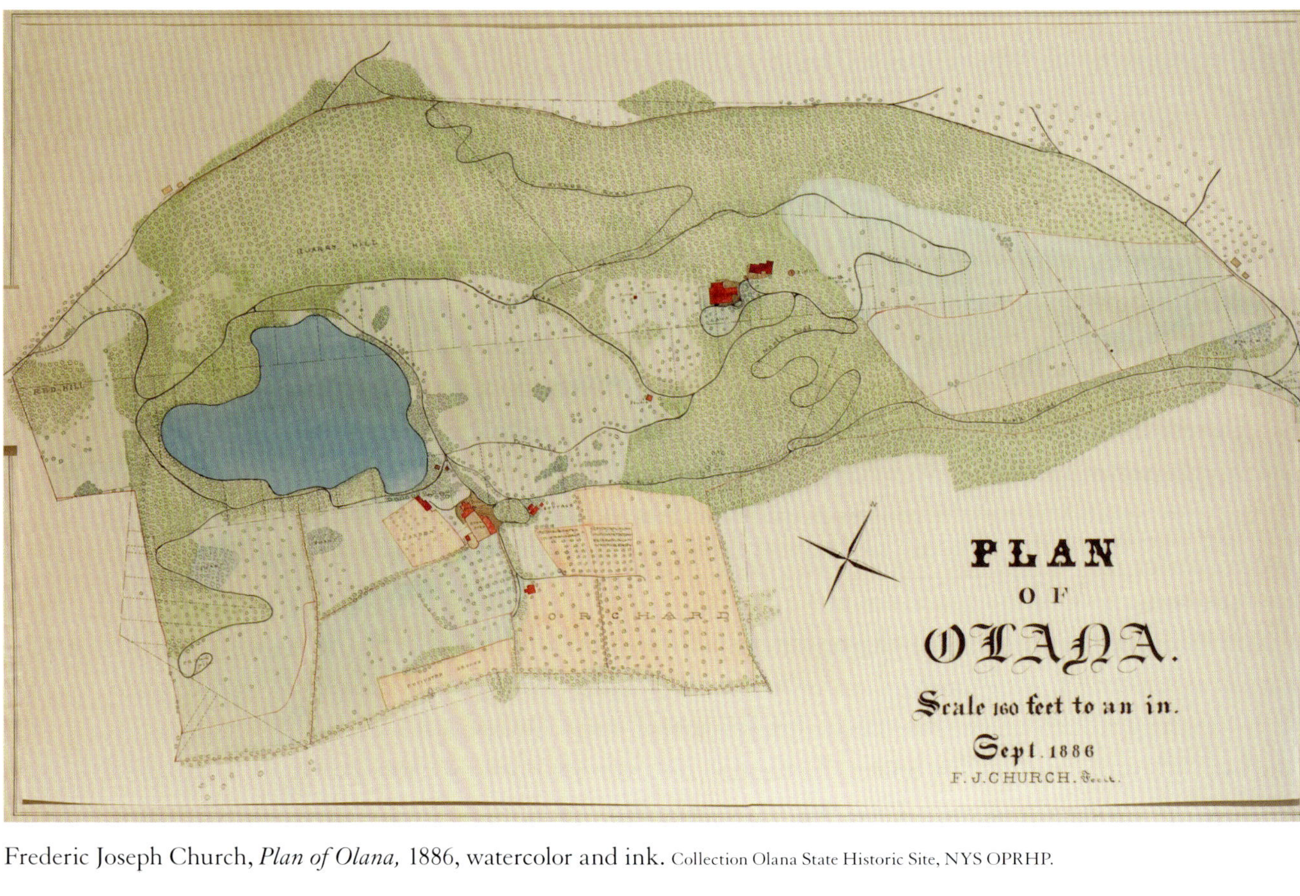

Frederic Joseph Church, *Plan of Olana,* 1886, watercolor and ink. Collection Olana State Historic Site, NYS OPRHP.

Vaux, *Study for a House for F. E. Church, Esq. at Hudson, N.Y.*, c. 1870, graphite on paper. Collection Olana State Historic Site, NYS OPRHP.

house, grounds, and drives that resembles the country park plans of his architect consultant. The manner in which roadways at Olana lead naturally to the destination of the house finds a precedent in Vaux's plan for Observatory Hill in Hillside Cemetery and at Prospect Park where the lookout tower was projected. Church also created a man-made lake to be viewed from the house, like those Vaux and Olmsted constructed in their parks. The present-day visitor to Olana who is familiar with the walks and drives in landscapes that Vaux planned cannot help but feel a certain kinship here with them.

But there may have also been a spiritual motivation in Church's design of Olana. His and Isabel's early years at the Farm were lived during the Civil War; many friends enlisted, and two died in battle. Their two young children, born in 1862 and 1864, both died of diphtheria in 1865. The art historian Karen Zukowski has suggested that we should view Olana as a kind of memorial place.[6] Expanding on this idea, Allegra K. Davis, associate curator at Olana, has observed: "In the landscape itself the use of picturesque carriage roads and gently curving topography,

Olana. Photo by Andy Olenick.

Olana State Historic Site. Photo by Peter Aaron/OTTO.

naturalistic woodlands alternating with open meadows, and even a reflective lake with a strategic distant view of the house and sky beyond mirror many of the features found in rural cemeteries." She proposes that "the house and its surrounding landscape also function as a monument to the many dearly departed of the Churches' lives. Here painted and physical landscapes of memory meet as spaces of solace and remembrance."[7]

Olana remained in the Church family until the 1960s. At that time, sale of the estate, which would have meant dispersal of the invaluable art collection and subdivision of the land, was avoided at the last minute when the State of New York agreed to purchase the house, its contents, and the grounds. Today Olana State Historic Site

View west from Olana (detail). Photo by Beth Schneck Photography.

is open to the public under the auspices of the state Office of Parks, Recreation and Historic Preservation with the support of the Olana Partnership. It is also honored as a National Historic Landmark. Guided by a 2015 Strategic Landscape Design Plan developed by Nelson Byrd Woltz Landscape Architects, the Olana Partnership and New York State Parks have restored the carriage road network that the Church family knew. In 2024 the Frederic Church Center for Art and Landscape, designed by Architecture Research Office in collaboration with NBW, opened as the gateway to the historic site, introducing visitors to Olana as a complete work of art, inside and out. As Adam Yarinsky, principal of ARO, explained, "every design decision was made with the landscape in mind, from the materials we selected to the way the building nestles into the site."[8]

View south over meadow, Olana. Photo by Lawrence Bridges.

View southward of Parliament Hill. Photo by Wladyslaw / Wikimedia.

Parliament Building, Ottawa, Ontario

(1873–1879)

On June 6, 1873, the Canadian secretary of public works directed Thomas Scott, the department's chief architect, to proceed to New York to "consult with the architect of the Central Park in regard to the projected laying out of the grounds of the Parliament Buildings here." Whether it was Scott's intention to visit Olmsted we will never know. If he had gone to see Olmsted, however, he may well have been told that the landscape architect was too busy to take on another project. Olmsted, who had just received the commission to design the grounds around the U.S. Capitol, had turned others away, pleading the press of current engagements. In any event, Scott met with Vaux, who warmly received him in his office at 110 Broadway.

Vaux spent two days with Scott discussing the project and taking him on a tour of Central Park, where he acquainted him with elements of the landscape that might bear on the Ottawa plan. Before Scott left the next day, he and Vaux had agreed on the "leading features" of a design. Within a few days, Vaux forwarded his "study for the arrangement of the grounds and terrace walls, in connection with the Government Buildings."[1] He also appended a "Plan for Ornamental Planting" and, a few days later, sent two partial revisions to the general scheme. Vaux also proposed that he visit Ottawa to make sure that all of his measurements were correct, but Scott and the Canadian officials failed to see the necessity of the expense.

Vaux's task was formidable: to unite into a single landscape composition three government buildings that occupied an elevated site, known as Parliament Hill, overlooking the Ottawa River. In 1859 the American architect Thomas Fuller had won a competition to design the new structures that would accommodate the House of Commons and Senate in the Parliament House and various administrative functions in two ancillary buildings, the East and West Blocks. The flamboyant High Victorian Gothic edifices, home to the new nation of the Dominion of Canada, formed a symmetrical ensemble that focused on the principal parliament building, which Fuller exalted with a soaring central tower, flanked on slightly lower ground by the East and West Blocks. The group faced Parliament Square, an as-yet-undefined open public space oriented toward the town, not the river. It was here that Vaux was to design a dignified setting for Fuller's buildings and bring them into visual harmony. Sloping ground added a considerable challenge.

Vaux's solution was an elegantly simple one. He emphasized both the existing symmetry of the buildings and the hierarchy of height. "As the Parliament House stands at a conspicuously higher level than the Department Buildings," he said, "it seems very desirable to make the whole arrangement of the ground seem to grow out of this controlling and somewhat peculiar circumstance of the site."[2] He proposed to create a terrace in front of the principal building that would be defined by an eight-foot-tall curved wall. A wide U-shaped carriage drive bordered the East and West Blocks and gently ascended to the terrace level in front of Parliament House. Pedestrians could approach directly from the street along a broad, straight path that traversed a spacious lawn. To frame the extended facade of Fuller's Parliament House, Vaux proposed to erect monumental flagpoles at either end of the terrace. Similar flagpoles had been part of his plan for the Bethesda Terrace in Central Park and would appear with similar purpose in Olmsted's 1875 plan for the grounds around

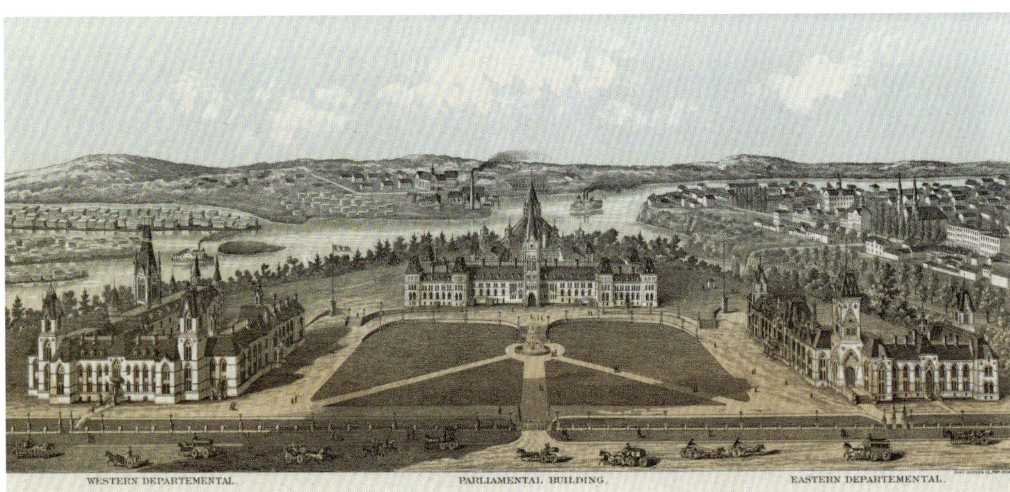

Government Buildings, Ottawa, Canada, tinted lithograph, c. 1865–80. Library of Congress Prints and Photographs Division.

Parliament buildings, Ottawa, 1901. Library of Congress Prints and Photographs Division.

Buffalo's city hall. (Olmsted would also include a terrace in his plans for the U.S. Capitol grounds.) Vaux's plan tied the buildings together in a monumental coherent unity, imparting the grandeur appropriate to such a significant public space.

For his work, Vaux received a one-time payment of five hundred dollars and the promise of one percent of construction costs upon implementation. The following May, however, the secretary of public works curtly informed him that "it is not the intention of the Government to carry out your design."[3] The matter would have rested there except that in 1876, Vaux learned that his plan was being built. By 1878 the project had been finished largely as Vaux had envisioned it. (The details of certain elements, such as the terrace wall, gates, and ironwork, were of others' design.) Vaux then petitioned the Canadian government for additional compensation; they responded positively in 1882. That year Vaux published a pamphlet recounting the troubling episode, the outcome of which he considered a triumph in his quest to achieve recognition of landscape architecture as a profession.[4] He would be gratified to know that the Public Grounds of the Parliament Buildings, including the Centre, East, and West Blocks and the Library, achieved status as a National Historic Site of Canada in 1976.

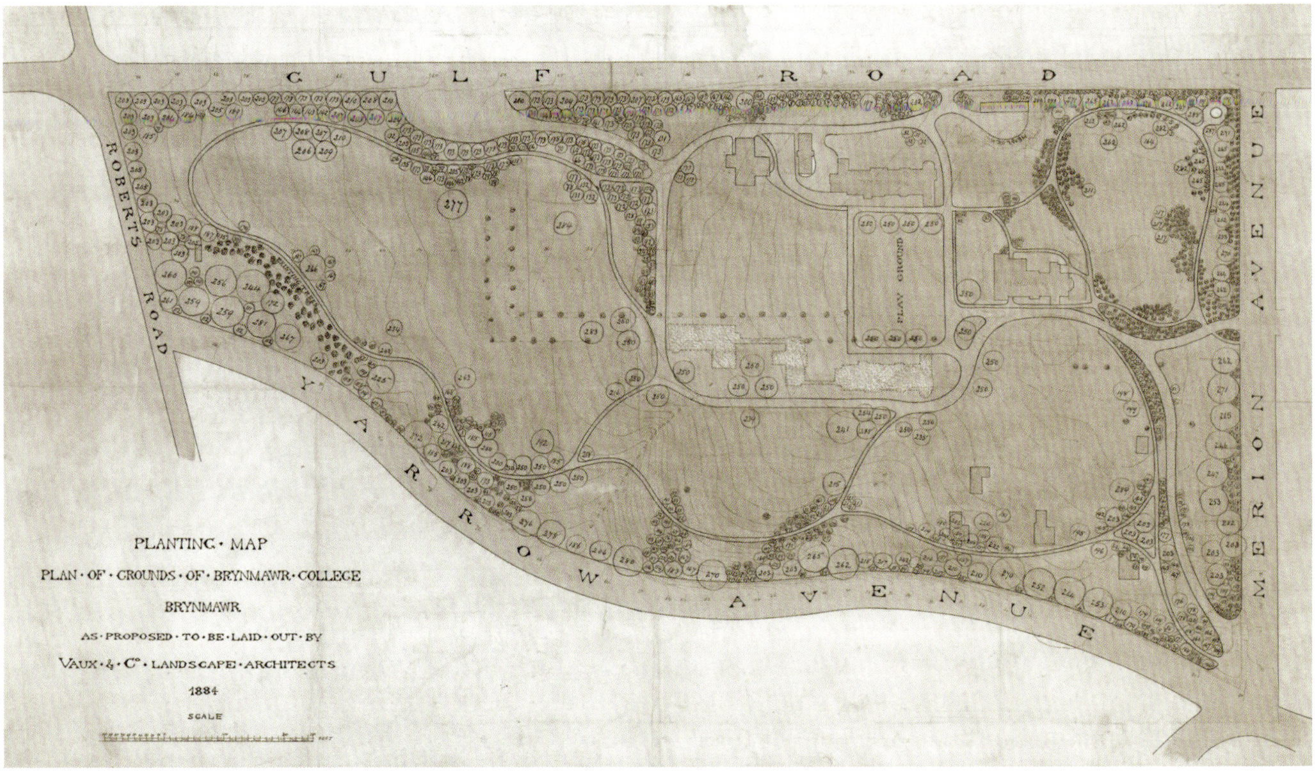

Vaux, *Planting Map / Plan of Grounds of Bryn Mawr College*, 1884. Courtesy Bryn Mawr College Libraries Special Collections.

Bryn Mawr College, Bryn Mawr, PA

(1882–1884)

In the 1870s, Dr. James Wright Taylor, a well-to-do Philadelphia physician and philanthropist, began promoting the establishment of a college for women under the auspices of the Religious Society of Friends. For its site he purchased forty acres outside the city in the picturesque village of Bryn Mawr (whose name, meaning "great hill," was given to the area by its first colonial settler, a Welsh Quaker). "It is a fascinating stretch of country," wrote a contemporary visitor, "full not only of fertility but of the fantastic wildness of real nature." The opening in 1869 of the Pennsylvania Railroad's Main Line and the construction of commuter stations had transformed the area into fashionable Philadelphia suburbs. Locals treasured the verdant woodland for its pleasant carriage drives, "many of them of surprising and romantic beauty, such as no stranger would expect almost within sight of a manufacturing centre of a million souls."[1] Among those who enjoyed life here was George Vaux, whose stone villa stood "on the edge of one of the wildest bits of woods within one hundred miles of Philadelphia."[2] George, a distant relative of Calvert Vaux, was a prominent Philadelphian who would become a benefactor of the new college.

Taylor enlisted Addison Hutton, a Quaker architect who had previously worked at nearby Haverford College, to erect two academic buildings on the highest point of the hilltop site. Construction began in the summer of 1879. There was, however, no thought of hiring a landscape architect to draw up a master plan for the grounds. Quite the opposite, as Hutten's view was that "the landscape gardener had little or nothing to do until the architect was pretty much through." An influential trustee echoed his sentiments, affirming that a landscape gardener should

"College (from Rosemont)." From Phillips Photographers, *Views of Bryn Mawr College* (1899). Courtesy Bryn Mawr College Libraries Special Collections.

not be allowed to "interfere with the architect in his efforts to embody the views of experienced College men touching important relations of the different buildings to each other."[3]

After Taylor's death in 1880, a former board member, James E. Rhoads, assumed presidency of the college. Rhoads's stewardship ushered in a more enlightened attitude toward the need for a comprehensive campus plan. In 1882 he dismissed Hutton and hired Calvert Vaux to create one, for which he would receive a fee of five hundred dollars. On September 29, Vaux's associate George Kent Radford presented the trustees with Vaux's preliminary design ideas, which included the previously determined building sites, with the exception of the contemplated gymnasium. Pleased with Vaux's "many excellent suggestions," including the better location for the gymnasium, the trustees approved his proposal. The following September, they reported that "a force of men have been at work on the lawn for some weeks under the direction of Vaux & Co., and much of it is now ready for the top dressing of soil." In March 1884, Vaux paid a visit to the campus bringing with him "a complete plan for the laying out of the College Grounds, with walks and drives recently completed," which the trustees formally approved.[4]

Vaux could draw on his earlier experiences with commissions for institutional campuses. Gallaudet College (now Gallaudet University), Amherst College, the Hudson River State Hospital, and the Buffalo State Hospital had all benefited from his participation with Olmsted in the layout of the grounds. Vassar College, which preceded Bryn Mawr as the first institution of higher education for women, had also sought the partners' counsel. A plan they formulated in 1868, however, seems never to have been implemented.[5] Vaux's plan for Bryn Mawr incorporated comfortable access to ample green space, emphasizing the elevated land where Hutton's buildings stood—towered Taylor Hall, the academic building, occupied the highest point—and the sloping hillside behind it. Along the perimeter of the triangular site, he planted a wall of trees and shrubs to screen the grounds from the surrounding world and to provide users with a feeling of pleasurable seclusion, as he and Olmsted had done along the edges of their parks.

Vaux placed the chief campus drive entrance some distance off to the side of Taylor Hall to avoid a straight-on approach to the main building. From the entrance, later known as the Pembroke Gate, a separate pedestrian path followed the curving carriageway that led visitors to Taylor Hall. This oblique view revealed the building to its best advantage, making it appear more a part of its pleasing

Carriageway and pedestrian path, 1896. Courtesy Bryn Mawr College Libraries Special Collections.

setting. (A secondary entrance a bit farther along the street gave access to a short walkway that led to the main path.)

On the lower ground to the west and south of the formal campus quadrangle on the hill, Vaux laid out a picturesque landscape for leisure that preserved something of the flavor of the vicinity's natural beauty. A sinuous path wound its way around the heavily planted border and encompassed a large open meadowland—the greensward that was invariably a major feature of Vaux and Olmsted's public parks. Thinking comprehensively, Vaux created a campus plan that seamlessly bound together the separate areas for learning and recreation.

Over the years, however, major changes to Vaux's campus were wrought as the college grew and new buildings were erected. A significant transformation took place in Vaux's lifetime, when, in 1894, the trustees contemplated an expansion of the property. They did not, however, consult Vaux. Instead, in June 1895 they asked Frederick Law Olmsted to advise them on future plans for the grounds. Soon after, Olmsted and his stepson and partner, John Charles Olmsted, came

Pembroke Arch, c. 1905. Photo by Will Aiken. Courtesy Bryn Mawr College Libraries Special Collections.

Exterior of Pembroke East, c. 1895–1929. Courtesy Bryn Mawr College Libraries Special Collections.

Old Gymnasium, c. 1897. Courtesy Bryn Mawr College Libraries Special Collections.

to Bryn Mawr to assess the situation. The following year, they presented their proposal, which the trustees accepted.[6] The Olmsted plan greatly enlarged the grounds on the west and south, doing away with the perimeter street that had defined the undulating hypotenuse of Vaux's compact design. It ushered in a new era of expansion that in later years consigned Vaux's concept, of a distinct academic area wedded to recreational space, to history.[7]

Grace Church, New York, postcard.

Grace Church, Manhattan

(1886)

In 1881 the socially conscious and well-to-do congregation of Grace Episcopal Church on Broadway at East Tenth Street in New York City commissioned Vaux to lay out the small plot of land that bounded the church and rectory, both dating from the 1840s, and the recently built social hall, Grace House, that stood between them. Vaux transformed the unprepossessing grounds into a tranquil garden inviting contemplation and repose amid the urban hustle. The Gothic-style church buildings, designed by James Renwick Jr., have been declared a National Historic Landmark. Although nothing of Vaux's plantings survive, we can draw a picture of his work from historic photographs and written descriptions, including Vaux's own account as well as comments by his protégé, Samuel Parsons Jr., who assisted him.

Vaux first addressed the existing path system, which, he said, was both unartistic and confusing. In place of the straight path that led directly from the street to the door of the rectory with branches to the basement and Grace House, he laid out two separate diagonally curving walks from the street to the rectory and to Grace House. A third path, concealed from view behind a hedge of California privet ("no plant thrives better . . . in smoke and dust, and under the peculiar stress of the city"), followed the north property line to a service entrance at the rectory basement. In this way, Vaux noted, "the walk system was reduced to a minimum required by actual convenience." He also relocated the sidewalk entrance a bit farther south "so that a considerable space of uninterrupted greensward might be left in front of the principle entrance door to the house."[1] These elements, and the iron fence along the sidewalk, do still exist.

Before beginning planting, Vaux prepared the ground to ensure it would sustain the new vegetation, especially through summer heat. In summertime, reflected heat from the surrounding buildings and streets subjected the garden to periods of excessive dryness. The soil, which was "of a sterile sandy character," was removed to a depth of eighteen inches and replaced with "fresh garden mould." As Parsons commented, "This deep culture is of prime importance in the construction of any good lawn, for only in this way can a permanently rich sod be obtained capable of enduring drought." When the new ground was regraded, Parsons reported, Vaux aimed at securing "a purely natural appearance, by making gentle knolls and undulations instead of abrupt angles and dead levels," subtle variations in surface so that "no part is left exactly level."[2]

To evoke a sense of spaciousness within the 100-by-60-foot grounds, Vaux used green lawn to unify the garden, which was, as Parsons described it, a "shallow basin of turf crowned or fringed with trees and shrubs."[3] Essential to the layout was the attention Vaux paid to visitors' viewpoints as they proceeded through the verdant space. "To the right of an observer approaching the rectory from the street," Vaux wrote, "the view was made to consist, first of a bay of turf extending almost to the angle formed by the transept of the church, and then, from another point in the walk, to a longer bay of turf that stretches as far to the east as the Grace House building will allow, the necessary emphasis of the best lines of view being secured by plantations of shrubbery that fringe the bays of turf without traversing them." Along the base of the buildings, Vaux insisted, "it is undesirable that shorn grass should be designed to run close up to the masonry work." Here it was better "to introduce, between the turf and the wall, an irregularly formed fringe of plants." In this interplay between greenery and architecture, he instructed, let Nature "be free to aid in giving a delicate variety of artistic decoration to this otherwise raw junction line."[4]

To achieve "delicate variety," Vaux composed the foundation plantings using tall and short flora with a rich diversity of foliage, his choices based on a close regard for texture, color, and shape. "Gradation in the height of the plants used is an element of success that must not be neglected," he wrote; "in this instance plants of a much lower habit of growth are introduced in connection with the fringe of shrubbery."[5] He relied on evergreens to furnish interest both summer and winter, thinking too that conifers worked well with the picturesque lines of Renwick's neo-medieval architecture.

Shrubs also played a role in year-round display. "As it was desirable to give a

Grace Church, street view, 1902, postcard.

somewhat evergreen character to the planting effects, the Tree Box was freely used in the new work," he explained. Vaux also favored rhododendrons, planting large specimens for "immediate effect." In addition, "the Azalea amoena was freely introduced taking its proper place in the design as a lower growth of somewhat similar character." Adding to the variety, "pyramidal birch was used in connection with the shrubbery groups. . . . The standard or bushy honeysuckles with clean vigorous leaves proved hardy and were used with good effect. The Kerrea Japonica with its neat attractive leaves served to make an agreeable contrast with the var-

Grace Church Rectory, 1911, postcard.

iegated leafed and dwarf Japan Quince. The delicate and feathery leaves of spirea thunbergii and the pyramidal variegated althea found suitable places in carrying out the design."[6]

Vaux continued his list of carefully selected species:

> The purple berberry was used here and there among the groups of foliage. Equally valuable in producing valuable contrasts were the dark green masses of berberis thunbergii. One of the most effective free growing shrubs used was the spirea apulifolia, which has large rich leaves, and is especially picturesque. This was here and there mingled with the privet, being suitable for the purpose, having a vigorous habit and strong outline. To add gray and silvery tints to the groups, the two species eleagnus hortensis and longipes were used. Hydrangea grandiflora, the great white and purple autumn

> flowering Japan hydrangeas, was also employed to advantage. Several varieties of mock oranges or Philadelphuses were planted in the larger growing masses of shrubbery; an attractive light green leaved Japan deciduous shrub, rhodotypos kerrioides, was also employed. Feathery masses of tamarix Indica and Africana were disposed at intervals among the other shrubs to lighten the general effect and to accentuate their skyline. The most beautiful background effect secured in connection with this arrangement of plants depended on the use of ampelopsis tricuspidata, or Japan ivy, which grew freely and rapidly clinging by fine rootlets close to the stone-work of the church and rectory.

Vaux conceded that "there was no suitable space in the grounds for the introduction of a comparatively large bed of bright flowers or leaf plants." An exception was the area opposite the front door of the rectory. There, color "had a definite value because it accentuated the line of separation between the close cut green of the lawn and the bluish gray pavement selected for the approach to the house." Parsons indicated that "a line of lower growth of bulbs, lilies, crocuses, and hyacinths, with herbaceous plants," was planned "to complete the landscape picture."[7]

In crafting the garden at Grace Church, Vaux orchestrated color, texture, and form according to the principles of simplicity and coherence. No matter how small a plot of ground may be, he maintained, above all, the observer should never experience any doubt "as to the reason of the introduction of the various accessories into the positions they occupy." The key to success is to pay "proper attention to the general laws of composition, requiring that the details should be related to the main design in a well-studied and intelligibly sequent way, and subordinated individually and collectively to some recognizable leading idea." This, he affirmed, is a universal rule that applies to "all other successful productions of an artistic character."[8] At Grace Church, Vaux created a small garden that presaged the tiny "vest-pocket" parks he would design a few years later for the tenement districts of New York City.

Canal Street Park, New York. From *Scribner's Magazine* (August 1892).

Small Parks, Manhattan

(1887–1888)

In 1887, after years of struggle by progressive reformers, the New York State legislature passed the Small Parks Act, which provided generous funding for the construction of small neighborhood parks in New York's crowded tenement districts. Passage of the act was politically motivated as well, as the historian Rachael Iannacone has noted. "Because parks and gardens symbolize a city's wealth and power," she observes, "politicians also rallied for more parks."[1] New York mayor Abraham S. Hewitt, a reform Democrat, vigorously promoted opening access to private squares and creating small parks below Fourteenth Street in Manhattan. As landscape architect to the Department of Public Parks, a position he assumed in 1888, Vaux, with the assistance of Samuel Parsons Jr., designed several in underserved immigrant neighborhoods.

Vaux looked to the neighborhood squares in Paris which had been opened to the public under Napoleon III. "The excellencies of the French landscape gardener's conception seem to be shown to the highest advantage in the public square or city garden," he remarked, "and the smaller it is the more apparent does the superiority of the Paris system become." He especially praised the Square de la Tour Saint-Jacques, opened in 1855, the first of the squares Haussmann had transformed into a small public garden. (It had necessitated the destruction of many houses to create a suitable setting for the tower of a medieval church that had been destroyed during the Revolution.) Vaux applauded its "inexplicable quality of attraction that belongs to works of the highest art, and transcends any street garden ideal that is likely to have been formed in the mind of a visitor who sees it for the first time."[2]

"Park at the Foot of Canal Street." From *In Old New York* (1894).

Vaux's Canal Park, the largest of his "vest-pocket" parks, opened in the autumn of 1889, reclaiming the long-abandoned site of a public market. Vaux's compact plan featured a broad, serpentine gravel path, lined on both sides with continuous rows of benches. A widened area near the center created a place where young children could play under the watchful eyes of mothers seated nearby. Sections of lawn behind the benches created a soothing green backdrop between the curving path and a border of shrubs (among them California privet, weigela, red-stemmed dogwood, and forsythia) that edged the grounds, which were bounded by an iron fence set into a molded brownstone base. The dense green border afforded visitors a pleasing sense of enclosure, a place sequestered from the noisy streets.[3] Trees planted along the wide sidewalk enhanced the screen and provided shade during the hot summer months. Beds of flowers, which Vaux considered inappropriate in his large pastoral parks, here brightened the diminutive landscape.

The little parks were expensive to maintain and, in addition, according to Samuel Parsons, required a policeman on duty most of the time. Parsons was pleased, however, to see how the public soon came to cherish these community places. Often, the users themselves guarded their maintenance and safety. "Before Mr. Hewitt carried through his enterprise of opening them," Parsons recalled, it was deemed impossible that the public would be able to use them without utter destruction coming to the shrubs, flowers, and grass. The mere friction of the passing multitude, it was thought, would ruin the grass borders. Three years of experience, however, has proved this belief to be a fallacy. People, as a rule, treat the place with respect, and often themselves reprimand grown-up people and children who seem likely to injure the grass or flowers. There is actually a guard set up by the neighbors, and to our surprise, the grass and flowers look as they do in Central Park.[4]

Vaux's design served those who frequented the area around the west end of Canal Street until 1921, when the park was razed during the construction of the Holland Tunnel. The erasure was to have been temporary, with the park to be reconstructed

Jackson Square Park. From *Scribner's Magazine* (July–December 1892).

several years later. Canal Park remained absent from the Manhattan map, however, until 2005. The $2.7 million restoration project, funded by a recalcitrant New York State Department of Transportation, strove to duplicate as much as possible Vaux's original conception.

Canal Park was one of several designs that Vaux, with Parsons's assistance, created for the triangular parcels formed at the juncture of converging streets in the oldest parts of the city. North of Fourteenth Street, the insistent grid-iron pattern of the Commissioners' Plan of 1811 prevails, and the triangular plots occur only at a few intersections of Broadway and the avenues. The first to be completed was Jackson Square Park, on a quarter acre of land located at the intersection of Greenwich Avenue, West Thirteenth Street, Fourth Avenue, and Gansevoort Street in Greenwich Village. In the early 1870s, the city improved the open space with plantings of grass and trees but had enclosed it with an iron fence that shut out the public. In 1888, however, after the mayor's push to open access to the city's parks, Vaux and Parsons created a new design, and in August, the gates to the park were unbolted. On the evening of the opening, an eyewitness, touched by the enthusiasm of the neighborhood's residents, chronicled the event:

> A great crowd assembled at the gateway before the gates were opened. They came down from every one of the streets that open into the square until strangers passing thought there was to be a mass-meeting. The crowd was made up of mothers and babies, some carried in their mothers' arms and some rolled in baby carriages; bare-legged boys, girls in their best dresses, young men and young women in couples, old and middle-aged men in their shirt sleeves and with pipes, and grandmothers in their caps and carrying their knitting. The seats ranged around the walk were filled in a few moments, and then the swarm of romping children and promenading sweethearts moving around the walk was so great that the park policeman had difficulty in pushing in among them. There was no music or illumination to celebrate the occasion, but the shouts and the hum of voices could be heard several blocks away, and the moon came up full and bright over the housetops and shed a broader light on the park than all the electric lamps in the neighborhood.[5]

The plan featured continuous benches along a ten-foot-wide asphalt path around the perimeter of the site, behind which a low barrier of shrubs screened sitters from the surrounding streets. A triangular section of lawn planted with trees and shrubs filled the center space, and a drinking fountain added another touch of civility as well.

The right-angle parcel bounded by Duane and Hudson Streets in Tribeca purchased by the city from Trinity Church in 1797 is the oldest dedicated public parkland in New York. After the commons had languished for many decades, in 1870, Montgomery Kellogg, parks department chief engineer, and Ignaz Anton Pilat, chief gardener, designed a new park of trees, shrubs, and lawn enclosed with an iron fence on a granite base. In 1887, as the city moved to open access to its parks, Vaux, with Parsons, implemented a more articulate plan for Duane Park featuring curving paths.[6] The twentieth century witnessed both the disappearance and the regeneration of the Vaux–Parsons design. In 1940 the WPA funded a classical-style makeover that paved much of the space with concrete. In 1999, however, a plan by the landscape architect Signe Nielsen returned the tiny park to the feeling of Vaux's day.

Designs for other small parks during this period included Abington Square (1888), Mulberry Bend (1889, now Columbus Park), Lincoln Square (c. 1890), and Rutgers Slip (1891). Vaux's Corlears Hook Park (1893) was the final small greenspace

Mulberry Bend, postcard.

Corlears Hook Park and Williamsburg Bridge, before 1908. Museum of the City of New York.

he designed. Creating the ten-acre park in the densely populated tenement district along the East River between Cherry, Jackson, South, and Corlears Streets required the demolition of businesses that had occupied the site for many years. The challenge was similar to what Vaux and Olmsted had faced at Niagara Falls (where Vaux continued to advise on the ongoing work). In the place of factories and stone and lumber yards, Vaux designed a verdant place of respite that included a large central area of lawn shaded by lindens and elms.

Seclusion from the surrounding streets, reported an enthusiastic commentator in *Garden and Forest,* "will be secured by lines of leafy trees, like Maples, along the outer boundaries, and among them strong-growing shrubs of such kinds as will thrive in densely populated portions of the city."[7] Street trees, some fifty feet apart, edged the curbs. Two shaded playgrounds, a music stand, and restrooms completed the program. From the roof of the comfort station, erected along the western edge of the park, Vaux invited visitors to enjoy a long view of the river, continually animated by the busy tide of floating traffic. "The plan seems admirably adapted to make the most of the situation," affirmed *Garden and Forest.* Vaux, however, did not live to see his work completed and appreciated. During the summer after his death, fifteen thousand people attended the park's opening ceremony. Already, Corlears Hook had become a "verdurous and refreshing spot."[8]

Downing Park, Newburgh. Photo by Daderot/Wikimedia.

Downing Park, Newburgh, NY

(1889; with F. L. Olmsted)

In 1887, two years after the death, at age eighty-two, of the noted pomologist Charles Downing, the City of Newburgh decided to honor him and his more famous late brother, Andrew Jackson Downing, by naming a new public park after them. Charles, Andrew's older sibling, "was always in complete sympathy with his gifted brother, and had many qualities in common with him," one obituary noted.[1] He had played an important role in the landscape gardener's early life and, after Andrew's death in 1852, had continued to keep his brother's legacy alive in horticultural circles with his many revised and expanded editions of *The Fruits and Fruit Trees of America* (1845).

Charles Downing had earned an international reputation for his studies of many varieties of apple trees. Charles Darwin corresponded with him and referred to Downing in *On the Origin of Species* as "an excellent horticulturist."[2] At the time of his death, a friend wrote that Charles Downing had devoted his long life "to the most peaceful and humanizing of all pursuits, the results of which have been a continuous blessing to his fellow countrymen, and carried his name and fame from his quiet home on the Hudson to every civilized nation wherein a love of the beautiful in nature maintains a foothold."[3] It was certainly fitting that public officials of the city where the renowned Downing brothers had lived and worked should memorialize them with a public park.

The city acquired twenty-five acres of elevated farmland with views of the Hudson River for the site. It was several blocks southwest of the nine-acre property that Samuel Downing had bought for his nursery when he came to Newburgh from

Massachusetts in the early nineteenth century. After his death, his estate was divided into two four-and-a-half-acre parcels for his two sons. Andrew's portion had become Highland Gardens; the other, Charles's lifelong home.

In 1889 the Newburgh city council engaged Vaux and Olmsted to lay out the new park. The collaboration, the last of their careers, had been fostered by Andrew's widow, Caroline Monell. For Vaux, Newburgh was a place filled with fond memories. It was here that he had begun his American career as Downing's partner, mar-

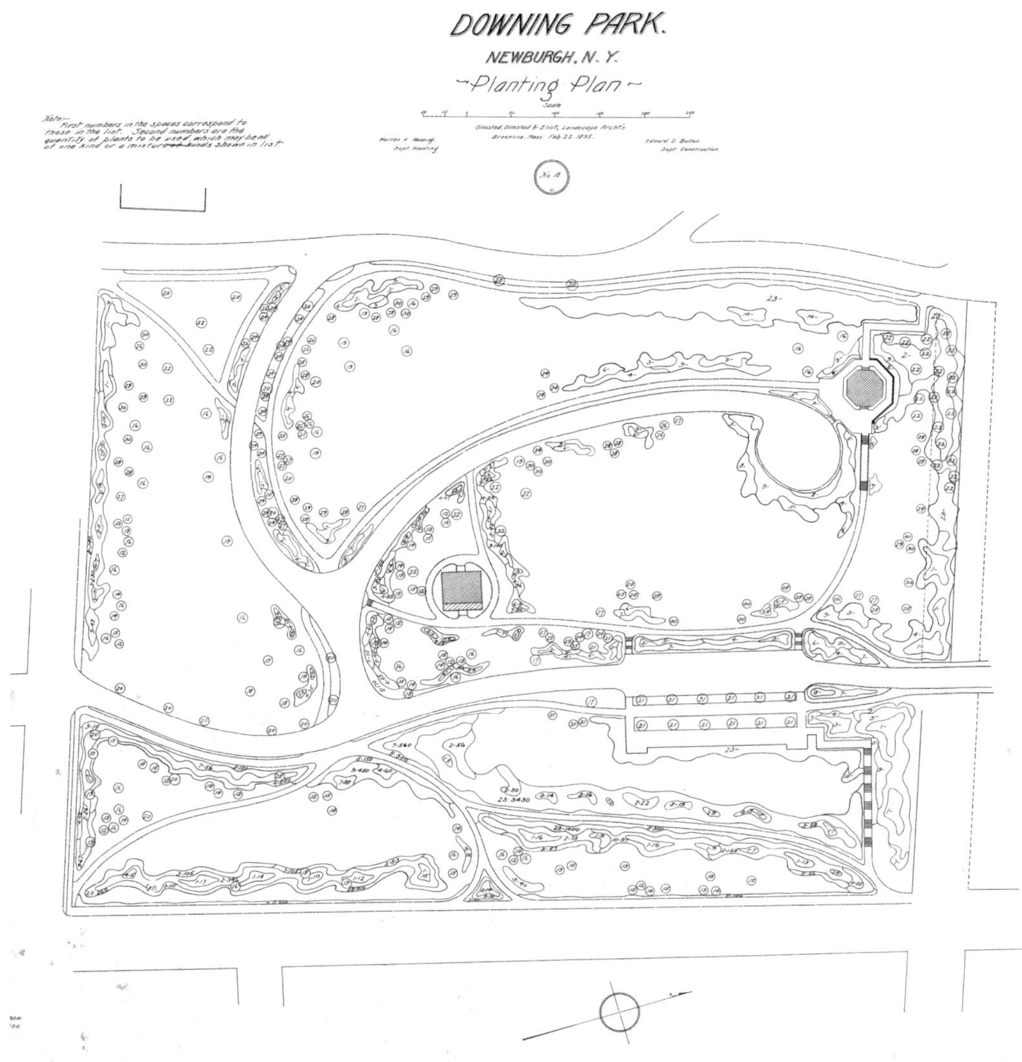

Olmsted, Olmsted & Eliot, *Downing Park. Planting Plan*, 1895. Courtesy National Park Service, Frederick Law Olmsted National Historic Site.

ried Mary McEntee, celebrated the birth of their three children, and maintained the office with Frederick Withers in which he had designed the many houses described in *Villas and Cottages*. Vaux also had many personal memories of both of the gifted brothers. It may have been Vaux who had asked Caroline Monell to convey to the city council his and Olmsted's offer to design the new park free of charge if it was named for the remarkable Downing brothers.

As they undertook their task in a renewed spirit of collaboration, the two men immediately realized that to create a proper park the city needed to increase the size of the site. Following Olmsted and Vaux's advice, the council ceded to the park ten additional acres that had been reserved for a reservoir adjacent to the western boundary of the original hilltop property. According to the late historian David Schuyler, Vaux took primary responsibility for laying out the steep eastern portion of the acreage. Olmsted concentrated his attention on turning the annexed lower western area into a lovely tree-studded meadow that included a large pond—popularly known as Polly Pond because of the many frogs that adopted it as their home. (In 1935 the city engaged the Newburgh architect Andrew Marvel to design a lakeside stone pavilion that became especially popular with wintertime skaters.)

In the eastern sector, Vaux laid out a carriage drive and pedestrian footpaths ascending to the summit of the knoll that was this section's chief feature. From here, visitors could enjoy a fine prospect of Newburgh Bay and the Highlands, with the

Entrance to Downing Park, postcard. Courtesy Joe Santacroce.

city's busy waterfront district in the foreground down the hill. The splendid scenic view echoed the one from Downing's Highland Gardens. To provide rest and shelter to visitors who climbed to the summit, an open-air brick-and-stucco pavilion, aptly known as the Observatory, was built according to a design by Vaux's son Downing. (The building no longer exists.) In their joint design for Downing Park, Vaux and

Carriage Drive, postcard. Courtesy Joe Santacroce.

Observatory in Downing Park, postcard. Courtesy Joe Santacroce.

View west over pond, postcard. Courtesy Joe Santacroce.

Olmsted succeeded in uniting into a seamless whole the two types of landscapes that Andrew Jackson Downing had extolled in his writings: the beautiful and the picturesque.

Construction stretched over several years, and neither Vaux nor Olmsted saw Downing Park when it officially opened in 1897. Vaux had died in December 1895. Olmsted's mental health had deteriorated, and he was confined to McLean Asylum. His stepson, John C. Olmsted, worked together with Downing Vaux to complete the job their fathers had begun—the only known collaboration between the sons of the two men who, inspired by Andrew Jackson Downing, had established the profession of landscape architecture on a firm footing in America. The park also signified that, owing to its two remarkable native sons, Andrew and Charles Downing, Newburgh held claim to an honored place in the rise of both the landscape arts and scientific horticulture.[4]

"A Place of about Seven Acres in a New Jersey Hill Town." From *Scribner's Magazine* (March 1892).

John H. Wisner House / The Clearing, Summit, NJ

(1889)

Beginning in the 1840s, the little village of Summit, New Jersey, located some twenty-four miles west of New York City, began to assume the character of a sought-after residential suburb. With its accessible rail connections and picturesque setting, Summit attracted a mix of middle-class and wealthy New Yorkers who built comfortable homes there. In 1879, Vaux designed a large frame house and studio for his artist friend Thomas Worthington Whittredge and his family. Whittredge's home took full advantage of the distant views offered by Summit's lofty location atop Second Watchung Mountain. The noted Hudson River School painter could contemplate the world as far away as New York City from the balcony of his belvedere dwelling.

The Colonial Revival house that the New York City architects Babb, Cook & Willard designed in Summit a decade later for John H. Wisner took advantage of another local natural feature. The Clearing, as the Wisners called their estate, was sited on the edge of a deep ravine, one of many glacial bowls that marked the irregular terrain of Summit. The estate offered enchanting views of native woodlands below. Whether Vaux's advice was sought in siting the house is not known. However, in the same year that the dwelling went up, the Wisners engaged Vaux, with Samuel Parsons Jr. at his side, to lay out the expansive seven-acre property.

Vaux approached the design aiming for minimal intervention that complemented his client's appreciation for the natural beauty of the setting. One of his first challenges was determining the best approach to the house from the public street about one hundred feet away. Because there was little level ground around the rim of the glacial bowl, the options were limited. Vaux chose to locate the entry to the property "on the extreme outside edge of the valley or bowl at a point nearest the highway," Parsons noted.[1] From there, the drive proceeded directly to the house. Fronted by a little stone terrace, the house was set on "a small level platform of made earth extending out to a sharp declivity." This narrow plot allowed "just enough space for the house and drive and a turnaround beyond it." Incoming carriages, after depositing their passengers at the front door, proceeded a short distance to the circular area where they might turn around. There could be no carriage drive beyond that point.

Considering the unusual lay of the land and the naturally picturesque woodland vale, Vaux judged that the treatment of the grounds should aim to reveal its natural treasures. He introduced open lawn only in front of the house so that residents and guests might enjoy a clear view of the charming green valley below. Starting at the far end of the carriage turnaround, a single footpath followed the perimeter rim of the forested property. At "many beautiful spots" along this gently winding way, the stroller was invited to pause and take pleasure in the natural scenes within the grounds. Except along the entrance drive and in front of the house, Vaux refrained

View of daffodils, n.d. Photo by Molly Davis. Smithsonian Institution, Archives of American Gardens, Maida Babson Adams American Garden Collection.

Reeves-Reed Arboretum. Photo by Daniel Case/Wikimedia.

from adding trees and shrubs. "The existing attractions of valley and native plantations," affirmed Parsons, "were greater than any that could be added, and additions would probably be somehow out of harmony with the naturalness of the scene."

The Clearing was acquired in 1916 by Summit residents Richard and Susan Reeves. They maintained Vaux's original landscape scheme intact until 1924, when they engaged the noted landscape architect Ellen Shipman and then Carl F. Pilat to make alterations to the property. Pilat, nephew of Ignaz Anton Pilat, chief gardener of Central Park, was landscape architect to the New York City parks department. Although the Reeveses rejected many elements of Shipman's plan, Pilat adapted her design for the Rock Garden (now Rock Pool) and is credited with the 1925 Rose Garden. Susan Reeves expanded the Wisners' original planting of daffodils down the slope into the bowl.

In 1968, Charles L. and Ann Reed bought The Clearing, adding an herb garden to the grounds and clearing woodland trails. Three years later, when they decided to move, the Reeds were instrumental in saving the estate from development by advocating for its conversion into a public educational arboretum. With the assistance of the City of Summit, funds were raised to preserve the land, and in 1974, The Clearing became the Reeves-Reed Arboretum. Today it is listed on both the National Register of Historic Places and the New Jersey Register of Historic Places.

Entrance drive, Wilderstein. Photo by Carol Betsch.

Robert B. Suckley House / Wilderstein, Rhinecliff, NY

(1890; with Downing Vaux)

In 1852, Thomas Holy Suckley, whose wealth derived from his astute speculation in the New York City real estate market, and his wife, Catharine Murray Bowne, descendants of two prominent Hudson River Valley families, purchased thirty-two acres of land along the Hudson near the village of Rhinebeck for their country home. The site, a former sheep meadow of varied terrain, afforded striking views of the river and the Catskill Mountains beyond. The same year the Suckleys engaged the New York City architect John W. Ritch to build a large Italianate villa at the most elevated spot. Ritch's 1848 volume, *The American Architect, Comprising Original Designs of Cheap Country and Village Residences,* showcased similar designs, and his assertion that "every handsome residence adds value, to the grounds attached to it; hence the importance of having such, by those who invest capital in this species of property" would have appealed as well.[1] They called their new home Wilderstein ("wild man's stone"), a name inspired by a Sepasco petroglyph found on the property.[2]

Thomas Suckley took as much pleasure in the scenic features of his estate as he did in the architecture of the house. A serious amateur horticulturist, he planted new trees on the mostly open landscape and was a careful steward of his land. When winter came, however, he and his wife returned to their apartment in New York City.

In the 1850s the popular composer Stephen Foster often visited the Suckleys at Wilderstein. Captivated by the picturesque setting, Foster fondly reminisced about his sojourns, especially the memory of his first. Having arrived by boat from New York City, he walked up the path from the dock, inhaling "the aromatic odor of the leaves" and listening to the "twitter of birds [that] alone broke the slumberous silence." On another occasion, he was pleased to be able to escape the torrid city for the Suckleys' country retreat. "Well, to Wilderstein we went, one bright and joyous summer day," he recalled. "The quiet of nature seemed to penetrate our souls as we approached the place." The setting was transporting: "We sat upon a rustic seat near the bank of the river, whose brightening waters reflected the splendors of the heavens above," he wrote. "The Catskill Mountains were steeped in heavenly light and clouds of gorgeous tints floated in the sky." Another time, "a violet hue had stolen over the river and its borders" as he was being summoned to tea. "How lovely that repast upon the piazza, in view of the river, the garden, and the lawn, with grand old trees scattered all over, breaking the uniformity, and increasing the richness and variety of the scene!"[3]

Thomas and Catharine Suckley were the first of three generations to live at Wilderstein, but the couple's years there were not always happy. Catharine died in 1879, and by the time of Thomas's death in 1888, only one of their several children had survived. Born in 1856, their second son, Robert Bowne Suckley, had grown

View through porte-cochere. Photo by Carol Betsch.

View from porch. Photo by Carol Betsch.

up in the enveloping landscape. In 1884 he married Elizabeth Philips Montgomery, who, like her mother, hailed from lofty Hudson River Valley lineage. The couple honeymooned for two years in Switzerland, returning in 1886 to settle in Orange, New Jersey. On his father's death, Robert became the sole owner of Wilderstein, as well as heir to a sizable fortune. He lost no time in completely remaking the sober Italianate villa he had known in his childhood into a Queen Anne–style mansion.

Robert instructed his architect, Arnout Cannon Jr. from nearby Poughkeepsie, to keep the original house but to more than double its size. "So radical was the transformation," notes Cynthia Owen Philip, historian of Wilderstein, "that it is difficult to believe the basic structure was retained."[4] The program included an added third floor, a five-story round tower with a ribbon-windowed uppermost level that served as a belvedere, and a broad, commodious veranda that embraced two sides of the ground floor. Cannon painted the exterior of the born-again manse in a vibrant crimson and green scheme. Likewise, the main interior rooms experienced a lavish transformation at the hands of Joseph Burr Tiffany, a cousin of the more famous Louis Comfort Tiffany. Gilded Age extravagance trumped Romantic-era gentility.

Neither did Robert neglect the landscape that had been so important to his par-

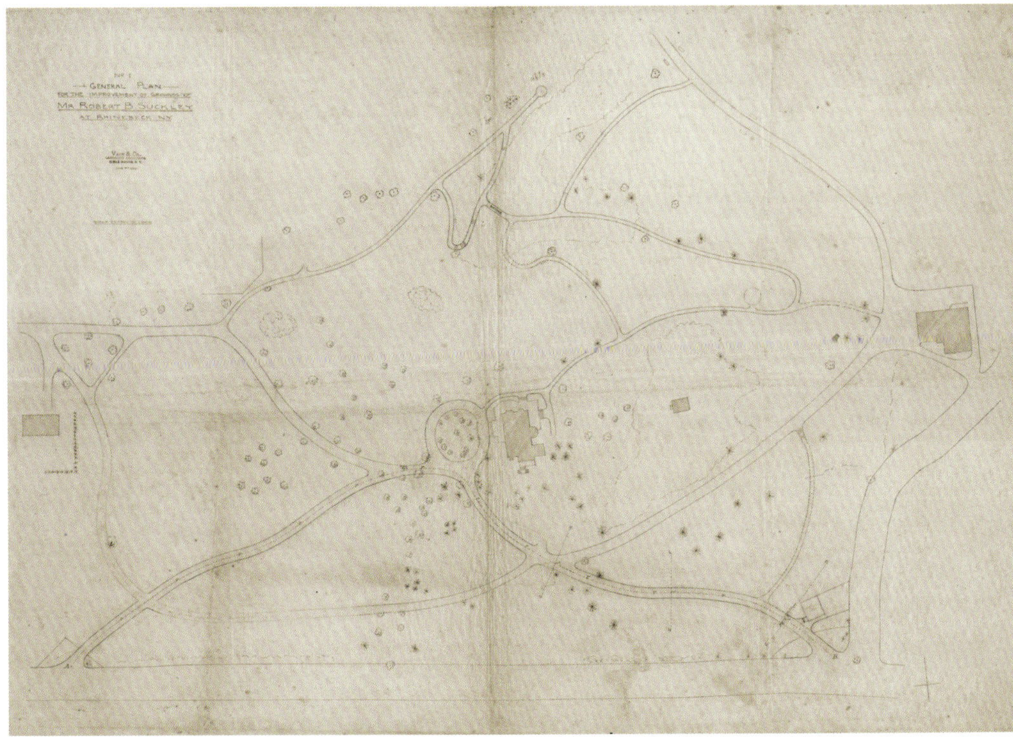

Vaux & Co., *General Plan for the Improvement of Grounds*, 1890. Courtesy Wilderstein Historic Site.

ents. Perhaps his honeymoon years in Switzerland had changed his taste in scenery. In 1890 he engaged Calvert Vaux to revise the layout of the property. Vaux made his first visit to Wilderstein in the company of his son Downing in April 1890. In November, Downing wrote to Robert that he, his father, and their associate Samuel Parsons Jr. were coming up to Wilderstein "in order to work up the planting for your place and decide on the trees we would advise you to cut."[5] Like Olmsted, Vaux espoused the judicious use of the axe when necessary to open vistas otherwise blocked by trees. The firm's final plan is dated 1891.

Respecting the natural contours of the land, Vaux's plan addressed the circulation needs of the thirty-two-acre estate. Fixing the mansion as the dominant element of his overall scheme (which incorporated some earlier roadways), Vaux laid out a winding circuit drive that loosely tracked the boundary of the irregularly shaped property. It provided carriage access to a new stable (the work of Arnout Cannon Jr.) at the northwest corner of the grounds and a riverside boathouse at Suckley Cove at the opposite end. A new gate lodge, designed by Downing Vaux, whose name appears on the drawings, was built at the entrance to the property at the public road.

From there a carriage drive traversed the grounds, past the house halfway along, to the river. Vaux likely advised on the siting of a large greenhouse (no longer standing), located discreetly out of sight along the eastern edge of the property.

These practical concerns notwithstanding, Vaux's plan for Wilderstein shared Thomas and Catharine Suckley's original intent to make the river scenery an attribute of the house. On the gently sloping land north and west of the mansion, Vaux proposed a series of connected footpaths with prospect points along the way inviting casual ramblers to pause and enjoy stunning views. He called for a summerhouse on a knoll along the path leading in the direction of the carriage house. At the point farthest from the house, Vaux erected a quaint wooden umbrella-like shelter. (A modern version marks the spot, known as Umbrella, or Mushroom, Point.) Like its earlier counterpart in the Ramble in Central Park, the rustic canopy signaled a wide viewshed. Here, a person might contemplate the river and mountains in one direction and the mansion in the other.

Because of Robert Suckley's able oversight of all the projects he undertook at Wilderstein, Vaux acknowledged that he could assume much of the responsibility for implementing his landscape plan. "The usual routine of practice when superintendence is undertaken," he told his exceptional client, "is to follow up the issue of such

Meadows and paths. Photo by Carol Betsch.

Path toward house. Photo by Carol Betsch.

View over front lawn. Photo by Carol Betsch.

a plan with visits repeated as often as may be required and costing the owner say $10.00 per day and expenses. . . . With your special knowledge, it would be expedient that you should supervise the work yourself at the outset as you could always let us know if any difficulty arose and we could send some one to meet it."[6]

Margaret Suckley, Robert and Elizabeth's daughter born in 1891, the year that Vaux presented the family his finished plan, grew up to be the most famous resident of Wilderstein. As a student at Bryn Mawr, perhaps she realized that the designer of the campus had also been the landscape architect for her home. Known by the nickname Daisy, she became the confidante of her distant cousin Franklin D. Roosevelt, serving as his personal archivist. Daisy Suckley continued to live her entire one hundred years at Wilderstein, and by establishing the nonprofit Wilderstein Preservation Inc. in 1980, she laid the foundation for the survival of the house and grounds as a public museum. In 1990, Wilderstein was designated a National Historic Landmark and, in 2007, joined the Hoyt House in the Hudson River Historic District listing in the National Register of Historic Places.

George Curtis, *Bridge to Luna Island,* 1895. Courtesy Rare Book Collection of the Buffalo & Erie County Public Library.

Niagara Reservation, Niagara Falls, NY

(1885–1895; with F. L. Olmsted)

During the 1870s and '80s, Vaux played an active role with Olmsted, Frederic Edwin Church, and others, including New York lieutenant governor William Dorsheimer, the father of the Buffalo park system, in the decades-long public campaign to persuade the New York legislature to set aside land at Niagara for a state reservation.[1] The natural wonder had drawn intrepid tourists and inspired awe since the early decades of the century. Church had visited the falls several times before he painted *Niagara* in 1857, the work that catapulted him to fame. Olmsted too had been an early visitor, first with his father in 1828, and again in 1868, when he and Vaux were in Buffalo working on the park system plan. In the years between, Niagara, privately owned, had become commercialized and the site of industrial development. Olmsted, distressed at what he saw, began to galvanize the effort to have the land protected.

Church was also a fervent supporter of the cause. "Some years since," Vaux wrote in 1878, "while Mr. F. E. Church was one of our Park Commissioners, he showed me in his studio an original sketch of Niagara, and the conversation naturally turned on its present disadvantageous surroundings both on the American and the Canadian side, and on the desirability of securing to the public all that was really essential to a full enjoyment of its beauties."[2] That year, in fact, Church approached Lord Dufferin, governor-general of Canada, with the suggestion of joint protection of Niagara. The proposal, which would aid in promoting friendly relations between the two countries, was publicly supported in a speech Dufferin gave as he left office.

Vaux and Olmsted believed that the experience of Niagara should encompass

John Frederick Kensett, *Niagara Falls,* c. 1852–54, oil on canvas.

not just the sublime magnitude of the thundering cataract but all the loveliness of the quiet scenery to be encountered in the land around the falls. Goat Island, which divided the river into two sections, the Horseshoe Falls on the Canadian side and the American Falls on the New York side, was to Olmsted the true treasure. Unlike the mainland shore, the island survived in an unspoiled natural condition, preserving old growth forest and a remarkable variety of native flora, but it too was being threatened by commercial development.

In 1883 former Buffalo mayor now governor Grover Cleveland, a close friend of Dorsheimer, established the Niagara Falls Preservation Commission. It marked a turning point in the battle for conservation. With Dorsheimer as its chair, the commission was charged with determining which lands New York State would acquire from private owners for the new public reservation. Working from the report Olmsted and James T. Gardiner, director of the New York State Survey, had presented in

1879, the commissioners decided to purchase the mainland shore, Bath Island, Goat Island, and Prospect Point.

In July 1883, Vaux urged them to "consider the whole subject in its more comprehensive aspects" and put forth a bold proposition. He wrote to Dorsheimer that "while returning from Niagara you asked me to send to you any suggestion that occurred to me. It is evident that the natural landscape boundaries of your projected reservation include the Niagara river, the rapids of the Horseshoe falls, the American falls, the Whirlpool rapids and the Whirlpool, beyond which point there seems to be no fresh incident of a salient character. The view down the river from the Whirlpool promontories is moreover of such ample scope, and its surroundings are so suggestive, that I cannot help considering the Whirlpool as the logical turning point in any general plan for preserving the scenery of the falls."[3] Dorsheimer, the consummate politician, however, while appreciating Vaux's desire to extend the boundaries of the park downriver to include the Whirlpool, strongly advised against it. He foresaw that asking too much from the Albany legislature—and Vaux's scheme also included a Whirlpool bridge to Canada—threatened to scuttle the entire undertaking. Heeding Dorsheimer's advice that the perfect was the enemy of the good, the commissioners rejected Vaux's suggestion.

George Wallis, *The Rapids above the American Falls,* 1853. Library of Congress Prints and Photographs Division.

Niagara-Falls, N.Y., 1882. Library of Congress Prints and Photographs Division.

Olmsted and Vaux, *General Plan for the Improvement of the State Reservation at Niagara,* 1887. Courtesy National Park Service, Frederick Law Olmsted National Historic Site.

Francis Lathrop, "Ideal View of the American Rapids after the Village Shore and Bath Island Are Restored." From *Special Report on the Preservation of the Scenery at Niagara Falls . . . 1879.* Courtesy Niagara Falls Public Library.

In 1885 the State of New York acquired the land and inaugurated the Niagara Reservation. After a long struggle, Olmsted, Vaux, Church, and their allies had realized their vision of freeing Niagara both from the grip of ugly development and from greedy commercial interests. The public was now able to view the falls without having to pay the high entry fees that had been charged by private owners. Two years later, the two gray eminences of American landscape architecture came together to devise a plan for the new park. "The commissioners seem to think," wrote the *New York Times,* "that the restoration of the river banks and the islands will never be complete till these have felt the magic touch of those famous landscape architects, Messrs. Olmsted and Vaux."[4] In Olmsted's view, it was "the most difficult problem in landscape architecture to do justice to, . . . the most serious—the furthest above shop work—that the world has yet had."[5] In this endeavor, he relied on Vaux's ability to size up a problem and devise a brilliant solution.

The result of this late collaboration was their 1887 *General Plan for the Improvement of the State Reservation at Niagara.* Their intent was to both restore and preserve the distinctive natural scenery around the falls and to make its unique beauty accessible to large numbers of visitors. They laid out a system of walks and drives that encouraged a leisurely experience of the trove of natural attractions that accompanied the spectacle of the falls themselves: rushing rapids, rising mists, sparkling reflections, rare wildflowers, old growth woodland, and numerous species of birds.

"Looking over the 'Whirlpool' and down the River—from the Canadian side," 1906. Library of Congress Prints and Photographs Division.

In Vaux and Olmsted's extensive text that accompanied the design, they summed up their guiding philosophy: "the one purpose for which the State invites the reservation to be visited—namely, the enjoyment of certain passages of natural scenery of a distinctive character—shall plainly control all the arrangements it makes."[6] Their aim was to emphasize nature over everything else. Anything commercial was to be prohibited. They also strenuously condemned the temptation to erect statuary. Citing as an example the Statue of Liberty, they directed that if "a costly object of art should be tendered to the State on the condition that it should be set up on Goat Island, the precept to which our argument has tended would be obliged with a declension of the gift as surely as it would the refusal of an offer to stock the island with poison ivy or with wolves or bears."[7] Even Vaux, who held a serious interest in the art of sculpture, had long maintained that the country parks that he and Olmsted designed were not places for memorials, no matter how high-minded or civic-spirited. Memorials, he believed, introduced sentiments and associations at odds with the prevailing pastoral mood and would clutter the landscape, distracting visitors from the simple experience of nature for which these grand greenspaces were created. In Olmsted's words, "appropriate places for all the monuments that will be erected can be found in the small parks and public squares, or open spaces here and there in the city, where they would show to advantage and not interfere with the view of broad landscapes."[8]

Olmsted and Vaux's plan consisted of several distinct areas that still inform the visitor's itinerary today. Prospect Point served as the main entrance to the grounds from the town of Niagara Falls. (Most visitors in Vaux's day arrived by train, walking to the park from the nearby station.) After the existing restaurants, dance halls, and bars had been removed, they laid out a series of walks that led to the spot where the best view of the falls could be had. Upriver from Prospect Point, along the area known as the Mainland Shore, many manufactories had been established to take advantage of the waterpower generated by the onrushing river. All were removed, and the shoreline replanted with trees and shrubs to create a naturalistic riparian environment. A carriage drive and footpath allowed visitors to enjoy the view of the American Rapids from the pleasantly shaded renewed shore.

On Goat Island, which was reached by an existing bridge from the mainland, there was no need to restore flora. A virgin forest covered the island, which botanists treasured for its unusually rich variety of native plant life. Olmsted and others regarded it as possessing the greatest number of species to be found anywhere in the eastern United States. He and Vaux proposed a carriage drive following the perimeter of the roughly triangular island with a footpath ringing the shoreline. The plan

View in the Primeval Woods on Goat Island, wood engraving after sketch by Thomas Moran, c. 1879. Author's collection.

First Sister Island bridge, 1894. Courtesy Niagara Falls Public Library.

Three Sisters Islands, c. 1890. Courtesy New York State Archives.

“Prospect Point in the New Park—Niagara,” c. 1880. Photo by George Barker. NYPL Digital Collections.

showed the location of numerous permanent stone benches with arrows indicating the direction of the scenic river views to be enjoyed from them. Walkers would also be able to stroll a network of paths within the woodland (although many were never built). Here, away from the roar of the falls, visitors were invited to take pleasure in viewing the flowers and listening to the birds. They might also walk out from the upper end of the island far into the Canadian Rapids via a series of bridges to the islets known as the Three Sisters and from there experience the torrents. Two small woodland shelters offering protection from sudden showers were the only buildings to be added to the islands’ landscape.

With their plan Vaux and Olmsted's primary intent was to increase people's awareness "of passages of natural scenery of a distinctive character."[9] Their vision was a more fitting setting for romance—honeymooning at the falls dates back to 1801, when Aaron Burr's daughter, Theodosia, and her husband, Joseph Alston, traveled to Niagara from New York City on their "Bridal Tour"—than the bustling, commercialized environment that engulfs and even intrudes into the park today.

Olmsted severed ties with the Reservation in 1888, perhaps because he disliked working again with Andrew Haswell Green, who assumed the commission presidency that year. Olmsted, who at the time was at the height of his career, may also have wished to give Vaux the opportunity to secure more income, for his partner was far less well off than the master of Fairsted. Indeed, Vaux & Co., Landscape Architects, served a very modest clientele compared with the nationwide reach of Olmsted's thriving firm. In any case, Vaux continued to be associated with the work at the Niagara Reservation until his death in 1895.

During that time, Vaux supervised construction and furnished plans for several

"Prospect Point, Niagara Falls," 1901–1902, postcard. NYPL Digital Collections.

structures and landscape accessories. One of these was the iron railing that replaced the clumsy masonry walls protecting visitors at Prospect Point and other precipitous locations throughout the grounds. Vaux's clever, minimalist design was a reassuring physical barrier that did not impede views of the expansive scenery. (Its modern aluminum counterpart evokes Vaux's precedent.) He modified the lines somewhat for the railing that wound alongside the curving stairs he designed to take visitors to and from Luna Island, a small piece of land on the brink of the American Falls. Its flowing sinuosity bound his stairs to the gently sloping hillside. Although today a straight

"American Falls & Niagara River," c. 1860–65. Photo by George Stacy. Library of Congress Prints and Photographs Division.

"Niagara Falls by Moonlight," c. 1885. Photo by George Barker. NYPL Digital Collections.

utilitarian flight of steps has replaced Vaux's structure, his First Sister Island bridge of 1894 still leads visitors to that unique sequence of islands. Built of rusticated blocks of stone quarried from the Niagara gorge, the gracefully arched span validates its picturesque surroundings. There was nothing new in this for Vaux. In the manner of his earlier Balcony Bridge in Central Park, Vaux built in protruding bays—one at one end of the bridge and two at the other end—that invited strollers to linger and enjoy the water and forest views.

At the close of his career, Vaux's involvement with the Niagara Reservation brought together many of the threads of his professional life: architecture, landscape architecture, collaboration with Olmsted, association with Andrew Haswell Green, affiliation with his son Downing—who designed a shelter on Goat Island—and devotion to a noble cause. He was able to apply his deeply held principles of landscape architecture to the conservation of natural scenery for the enjoyment and uplift of all of us.

Notes

Overview

1. Olmsted to Paul Dana, March 12, 1891, Olmsted Associates Records: Letterbooks, 1884–1899, 1891, March 2–April 20, Library of Congress.
2. "Death of Calvert Vaux, Landscape Architect," *American Architect and Building News* 50 (November 30, 1895): 93.
3. Jennifer Thomas, "The Insane Asylum Landscapes of Olmsted and Vaux," article 15 in Olmsteds: Landscapes and Legacies series, National Park Service, 2022. PDF available at https://www.nps.gov/articles/.
4. Olmsted to Mary Olmsted, September 15, 1862, Frederick Law Olmsted Papers, Manuscript Division, Library of Congress, Washington, DC (hereafter FLO Papers).
5. Quoted in David Schuyler, *Apostle of Taste: Andrew Jackson Downing, 1815–1852* (1996; repr., Amherst: Library of American Landscape History, 2015), 78–79.
6. All of these properties are listed in the National Register of Historic Places. Ammadelle is a National Historic Landmark.
7. Kerry Dean Carso, *Follies in America: A History of Garden and Park Architecture* (Ithaca, NY: Cornell University Press, 2021), 1.
8. Vaux to Clarence Cook, June 6, 1865, Calvert Vaux Papers, Manuscripts and Archives Division, New York Public Library.
9. "Calvert Vaux Missing," *New-York Times,* November 21, 1895.
10. Mary Olmsted to John C. Olmsted, October 24, 1878, FLO Papers.
11. Isaac Taylor, *Home Education* (London: Jackson and Walford, 1838), 48.
12. Edgar Mayhew Bacon, *The Hudson from Ocean to Source* (New York: G. P. Putnam's Sons, 1902), 277.
13. Ibid.
14. William Cullen Bryant, *Picturesque America,* 2 vols. (New York: D. Appleton, 1872), 2:6.
15. David Schuyler, *Sanctified Landscape: Writers, Artists, and the Hudson River Valley, 1820–1909*

(Ithaca, NY: Cornell University Press, 2012), 3. The exhibition *Great Green Hope for the Urban Blues: Art and Myths of the Hudson Valley* (Frances Lehman Loeb Art Center, Vassar College, 2025) explored the ways the "enduring pastoral myth" of the Hudson River Valley obscures the historical realities of the region.

16. Calvert Vaux, *Villas and Cottages* (New York: Harper & Brothers, 1857), 38.
17. Vaux to Olmsted, July 6, 1865, in *The California Frontier, 1863–1865,* ed. Victoria Post Ranney, vol. 5 of *The Papers of Frederick Law Olmsted* (Baltimore: Johns Hopkins University Press, 1990), 402 (hereafter cited as *Papers of FLO,* 5).
18. Vaux, *Villas and Cottages,* 277.
19. Henry Winthrop Sargent, *Skelton Tours* (New York: Appleton, 1871), 4.
20. Henry Winthrop Sargent, "Supplement," in A. J. Downing, *Treatise on the Theory and Practice of Landscape Gardening,* 6th ed. (New York: C. M. Saxton, Barker, 1859), 440.
21. Unfortunately, nothing remains of this fully evolved expression of Romantic-era home life. Fire destroyed the house in the 1930s, and two decades later developers divided the grounds for residential building lots.
22. Vaux, *Villas and Cottages,* vi.
23. Andrew Jackson Downing, March 3, 1851, "Explanatory Notes," quoted in Wilcomb E. Washburn, "Vision of Life for the Mall," *AIA Journal* 47 (March 1967): 53.
24. *Journals of Ralph Waldo Emerson,* ed. E. W. Emerson and W. E. Forbes (Cambridge, MA: Riverside Press, 1909–1914), vol. 8, 574.
25. The vase was carved by the Russian American sculptor Robert Eberhard Launitz and featured in Vaux's *Villas and Cottages.*
26. In addition to sons Bowyer and Downing, the Vauxes had two daughters: Julia, born in 1858, and Marian, born 1864.
27. For a magisterial history of the land and its inhabitants, see Sara Cedar Miller, *Before Central Park* (New York: Columbia University Press, 2022).
28. Olmsted to Mariana Griswold Van Rensselaer, June 11, 1893, in *The Years of Olmsted, Vaux & Co., 1865–1882,* ed. David Schuyler and Jane Turner Censer, vol. 6 of *The Papers of Frederick Law Olmsted* (Baltimore: Johns Hopkins University Press, 1992), 609 n. 8 (hereafter cited as *Papers of FLO,* 6).
29. Samuel Parsons Jr., "History of the Development of Central Park," *Proceedings of the New York State Historical Association* 7 (1919), 167.
30. Vaux to Olmsted, May 22, 1865, in *Papers of FLO,* 5:376.
31. George B. Tatum, introduction to William Alex, *Calvert Vaux, Architect & Planner* (New York: INK, 1994), 30.
32. "Consolidation Jan. 1, 1898 . . . Mr. Green's Tribute to Calvert Vaux," *New-York Times,* January 7, 1896.
33. Allan Nevins and Milton Thomas, eds., *The Diary of George Templeton Strong,* 4 vols. (New York: Macmillan, 1952), 4:385.
34. Mabel Parsons, ed., *Memories of Samuel Parsons: Landscape Architect of the Department of Public Parks, New York* (New York: G. P. Putnam's Sons, 1926), 126.

35. Vaux to Olmsted, May 10, 1865, in *Papers of FLO,* 5:359.
36. Vaux to Olmsted, July 8, 1865, ibid., 404.
37. Ibid.
38. Vaux to Olmsted, June 3, [1865], ibid., 387.
39. Vaux to Olmsted, July 6, 1865, FLO Papers.
40. Vaux to Olmsted, July 8, 1865, in *Papers of FLO*, 5: 404.
41. Calvert Vaux, "A National Park at Niagara," Letters from the People, *New-York Tribune,* October 5, 1878.
42. Olmsted to Mariana Griswold Van Rensselaer, May 22, 1893, FLO Papers.
43. Olmsted to Alfred J. Bloor, October 4, 1882, in *Papers of FLO,* 6:37.
44. Vaux's quixotic London compatriot Jacob Wrey Mould (1825–1886) often contributed decorative elements to his designs. Held in high esteem by his contemporaries, Mould, like Vaux, excelled as a draftsman, and his many resplendent drawings preserved in the New York City Municipal Archives confirm his exceptional talent. I review Mould's career in *Hell on Color, Sweet on Song: Jacob Wrey Mould and the Artful Beauty of Central Park,* with Lucille Gordon (New York: Fordham University Press, 2023).
45. Esther da Costa Meyer, *Dividing Paris: Urban Renewal and Social Inequality, 1852–1870* (Princeton, NJ: Princeton University Press, 2022), 230.
46. Calvert Vaux, "The Parks and Gardens of Paris," in Calvert Vaux and Samuel Parsons Jr., *Concerning Lawn Planting* (New York: Orange Judd, 1881), 15.
47. "Good Progress on the Tomb," *New-York Times,* August 1, 1885.
48. "Mr. Olmsted's Ultimatum," *New-York Tribune,* November 24, 1894.
49. Samuel Parsons Jr., *The Art of Landscape Architecture* (1915; repr., Amherst: Library of American Landscape History, 2009), xii.
50. "The Central Park Plan. Mr. Calvert Vaux's Part in It. To the Editor of the Tribune," *New-York Tribune,* February 18, 1878.
51. [C. S. Sargent], "A Botanic Garden for the City of New York," *Garden and Forest* 5 (December 26, 1888): 517.
52. "Bronx Park," *Garden and Forest* 4 (July 1891): 314.
53. New York Department of Public Parks, *Annual Report,* January 1895, 5.
54. "Park Notes," *Park and Cemetery* 5 (March 1895): 105. Today, hemlock woolly adelgid has devastated much of the forest Vaux admired. Nevertheless, Eric Sanderson of the Wildlife Conservation Society at the Bronx Zoo says that "the forest at the New York Botanical Garden is revelatory. I believe it's the only substantial patch of old growth forest left in the city." Quoted in Michael Kimmelman, *The Intimate City: Walking New York* (New York: Penguin Press, 2022), 243.
55. Gregory Long, *Rescue and Revival: New York Botanical Garden, 1989–2018* (Amherst: Library of American Landscape History, 2022), 140. As director of NYBG, Long oversaw the restoration and renaissance of the institution.
56. New York Department of Public Parks, *Annual Report,* January 1896, 5.
57. Vaux, "The Parks and Gardens of Paris," 17.

58. Vaux, *Villas and Cottages,* 214, 55.
59. Ibid., 193–94.
60. Ibid., 282, 248, 129.
61. Ibid., 53.
62. Ibid., 54.
63. Ibid., 51, 56.
64. Ibid., 278.
65. Calvert Vaux, "A National Park at Niagara," in Vaux and Parsons Jr., *Concerning Lawn Planting,* 36.
66. Ibid.
67. Calvert Vaux, "Nature and Art in Lawn Planting," ibid., 11.
68. James Jackson Jarves, *The Art-Idea: Sculpture, Painting, and Architecture in America,* 5th ed. (Boston: Houghton Mifflin, 1864), 316.
69. Vaux, "A National Park at Niagara."
70. Edmund C. Stedman, *Octavius Brooks Frothingham and the New Faith* (New York: G. P. Putnam's Sons, 1876), 19.
71. Vaux *Villas and Cottages,* 155.
72. Ibid., 154.
73. Calvert Vaux, "The Palisades," The Fraternity Papers (1878), New-York Historical Society.
74. The overlook may have been Vaux's own construction. For a time in the 1870s, he lived above the Palisades at Alpine, NJ, where he seems to have been involved in planning a residential community that, like Chicago's Riverside, would have comprised both private and communal lands.
75. Calvert Vaux, "Sky and Sky Line," in Vaux and Parsons Jr., *Concerning Lawn Planting,* 7–8.
76. Ibid.
77. Vaux, *Villas and Cottages,* 40.
78. Ibid.
79. Ibid., 291–92.
80. Ibid., 242–43.
81. Calvert Vaux, "Hints for Country House Builders," *Harper's New Monthly Magazine* 11 (November 1855): 764.
82. Vaux, *Villas and Cottages,* 40.
83. Vaux, "Hints for Country House Builders," 764.
84. Vaux to Olmsted, July 8, 1865, FLO Papers.
85. Bremer W. Pond, "Fifty Years in Retrospect: Brief Account of the Origin and Development of the ASLA," *Landscape Architecture Magazine* 40 (January 1950): 60.
86. Joy M. Kestenbaum, "Downing Vaux (1856–1926)," in *Pioneers of American Landscape Design,* ed. Charles A. Birnbaum and Robin Karson (New York: McGraw-Hill, 2000), 412.
87. "Calvert Vaux Dead," *New York Herald,* November 22, 1895.
88. Samuel Parsons and W. R. O'Donovan, "The Art of Landscape Gardening in Central Park," *Outlook* 84 (September 22, 1906): 230.
89. Parsons, ed., *Memories of Samuel Parsons,* 123.

90. Ibid., 4.
91. Vaux, "A National Park at Niagara."
92. "Consolidation Jan. 1, 1898 . . . Mr. Green's Tribute to Calvert Vaux."

Lydig and Geraldine Hoyt House / The Point, Staatsburg, NY

1. Calvert Vaux, *Villas and Cottages* (New York: Harper & Brothers, 1857), 283.
2. The landscape historians Emily Cooperman and Kyle Toth have recounted how Vaux applied his deep knowledge of the picturesque to the problem of siting the house in this striking setting. See their "Realizing the Picturesque: The American Landscape, Calvert Vaux, and The Point," *Hudson River Valley Review* 39, no. 1 (Autumn 2022): 48–59. Their research, undertaken for the Calvert Vaux Preservation Alliance, was adapted in 2024 to a narrative, "Touring the Point: A Picturesque American Landscape Experience," available at https://www.calvertvaux.org/news. Earlier studies of the Hoyt House are Joy Kestenbaum, *Historical Analysis of the Hoyt House, Mills-Norrie State Park, Staatsburg, NY* (Albany: New York Office of Parks, Recreation and Historic Preservation, n.d.), and Doell & Doell, *A Landscape Management Plan for "The Point"* (Syracuse, NY, 1998). In 1993 the New York secretary of state designated The Point and adjoining lands as a Scenic Area of Statewide Significance under provisions of the Coastal Management Act.
3. A.G.S., *In Memory of Two Sisters, Angelica Livingston Hamilton (Died April 21st, 1896) and Geraldine Livingston Hoyt (Died April 17th, 1897)* (New York: privately printed, 1897), 35.
4. Vaux, *Villas and Cottages,* 284.
5. Ibid.

Central Park, Manhattan

1. "Samuel Parsons, "History of the Development of Central Park," *Proceedings of the New York State Historical Association* 17 (1919): 168.
2. Olmsted, Vaux & Co., *Preliminary Report upon the Proposed Suburban Village at Riverside, Near Chicago. New York: September 1, 1868,* in *Papers of FLO,* 6:287.
3. *Tenth Annual Report of the Board of Commissioners of the Central Park for the Year Ending December 31, 1867,* 39.
4. Sara Cedar Miller, *Before Central Park* (New York: Columbia University Press, 2022), 5.
5. Edward Hagaman Hall, "History of Central Park in the City of New York," *Sixteenth Annual Report of the American Scenic and Historic Preservation Society* (Albany, 1911): 470.
6. See Sara Cedar Miller, *Central Park, An American Masterpiece: A Comprehensive History of the Nation's First Urban Park* (New York: Abrams, 2003), 245 n. 26.
7. Samuel Parsons, *Landscape Gardening Studies* (New York: John Lane, 1910), 14–15.
8. Samuel Parsons Jr., *The Art of Landscape Architecture* (1915; repr., Amherst: Library of American Landscape History, 2009), 242.
9. Paul Goldberger, *The City Observed, New York: A Guide to the Architecture of Manhattan* (New York: Vintage, 1979), 189.

10. Vaux to Clarence Cook, June 6, 1865, Calvert Vaux Papers, Manuscripts and Archives Division, New York Public Library.
11. Kerry Dean Carso, *Follies in America: A History of Garden and Park Architecture* (Ithaca, NY: Cornell University Press, 2021), 84.
12. In 1890, when commissioners proposed a new sandy playground on a sloping site west of the Dairy and the Kinderberg, the plan included a grand playhouse that Vaux designed to span the Sixty-Fourth Street transverse road. Yet Vaux was ambivalent about the undertaking. His friend Paul Dana told Olmsted that it was "difficult to get his exact feeling on the subject, but unquestionably he considers the project upon the ground of expediency and as a means of heading off something else which might be more undesirable." Dana to Olmsted, February 24, 1891, FLO Papers. Vaux foresaw especially that the sand would frequently wash away, resulting in the need for constant maintenance. Eventually the idea was dropped.
13. Kate Colquhoun, *The Busiest Man in England: The Life of Joseph Paxton, Gardener, Architect, and Victorian Visionary* (Boston: David R. Godine, 2003), 112.
14. George F. Chadwick, *The Works of Sir Joseph Paxton, 1803–1865* (London: Architectural Press, 1961), 53–54.
15. Clarence Cook, "Central Park," *Scribner's Monthly* 6 (September 1873): 535–36.
16. Parsons, *Art of Landscape Architecture*, 291.
17. The Central Park Conservancy has worked to reconstruct the Kinderberg arbor (demolished in the 1940s and substantially rebuilt in 2023), the Umbrella Seat, and several other of Vaux's rustic constructions. The summerhouse in the Dene ("valley") has been reproduced and restored to its position atop a large rock outcropping at Sixty-Seventh Street and Fifth Avenue, and a similar re-created polygonal summerhouse once again overlooks the southern border of the park.
18. Calvert Vaux, Frederic Church, and Henry Stebbins, *Report of the Committee on Statues in the Park, 25 April 1873,* in Frederick Law Olmsted Jr. and Theodora Kimball, eds., *Frederick Law Olmsted, Landscape Architect, 1822–1903: Forty Years of Landscape Architecture,* 2 vols. (1922–28; repr., New York: Blom, 1970), 2:489.
19. H. Van Buren Magonigle, "A Half a Century of Architecture, I: A Biographical Review," *Pencil Points* 14 (November 1933): 477.
20. "Calvert Vaux," *The National Cyclopedia of American Biography,* vol. 9 (New York: James T. White, 1899), 333.
21. Jervis McEntee, May 7, 1886, Jervis McEntee Diaries, Archives of American Art, Smithsonian Institution.
22. "An English Writer" [William Robinson], quoted in Parsons, *Art of Landscape Architecture*, 288.
23. Cook, "Central Park," 532.

Hillside Cemetery, Middletown, NY

1. "Obituary: James N. Pronk," *The Argus* (Middletown), October 16, 1895.
2. Ibid.

3. Ibid.
4. Diary of Alfred Janson Bloor, February 13, 1861, The New York Historical. Bloor also related that there had been some unspecified suggestions from Olmsted. See also Louis Van Orden Mills, *A History of Hillside Cemetery and the Community It Serves* (Middletown, NY: Hillside Cemetery Corporation, 2003), and JoEllen Hundeland, *Hillside Cemetery, Middletown, New York: Beyond the Graves* (Havertown, PA: America Through Time, 2023).
5. "The Cemetery of the Evergreens," *Brooklyn Daily Eagle,* September 28, 1850. In the 1880s, Vaux, together with Samuel Parsons Jr., would be hired to design an addition to Evergreens Cemetery, following the principles of the so-called lawn cemetery style that they espoused.
6. A copy of Chickering's map was held in the office of Benedict Memorials, Middletown, but it has since disappeared. Mills, *History of Hillside Cemetery*, 8.
7. Kerry Dean Carso, *Follies in America: A History of Garden and Park Architecture* (Ithaca, NY: Cornell University Press, 2021), 75.
8. Dieter Kienast quoted in Anette Freytag, *The Landscapes of Dieter Kienast* (Zurich: gta Verlag, 2021), 282. Hillside Cemetery was listed in the National Register of Historic Places in 1994.

Prospect Park, Brooklyn

1. A. J. Bloor, "Letters to the Editor," *New-York Tribune,* September 19, 1903.
2. David P. Colley, *Prospect Park, Olmsted & Vaux's Brooklyn Masterpiece* (New York: Princeton Architectural Press, 2013), 43.
3. Charles E. Beveridge, *Frederick Law Olmsted: Plans and Views of Public Parks,* ed. Charles E. Beveridge et al., vol. 2 of *The Papers of Frederick Law Olmsted,* supp. series (Baltimore: Johns Hopkins University Press, 2015), 74.
4. "Prospect Park," *Brooklyn Daily Union,* January 30, 1866.
5. "Prospect Park—Tangible Progress," ibid., January 31, 1866.
6. "Prospect Park, The Plan of Messrs. Olmsted and Vaux," ibid., March 20, 1866.
7. "Prospect Park: The Fountain at the Plaza," *Brooklyn Daily Eagle,* June 2, 1874.
8. Ibid. In 1897 the city replaced Vaux's creation with the Electric Fountain and in 1932 installed the Bailey Fountain, in place today.
9. "Prospect Park: Rambling of President Stranahan," *Brooklyn Daily Eagle,* June 2, 1874.
10. William Cullen Bryant, ed., *Picturesque America; or, The Land We Live In,* 2 vols. (New York: D. Appleton, 1872), 2:561–62.

Riverside, IL

1. "Founding a Town," *Chicago Evening Post,* December 31, 1869.
2. A detailed explanation of Riverside's original sanitary engineering was reported ibid.
3. Kate Colquhoun, *The Busiest Man in England: The Life of Joseph Paxton, Gardener, Architect, and Victorian Visionary* (Boston: David R. Godine, 2003), 112.
4. Olmsted, Vaux & Company to the Riverside Improvement Company, December 1, 1868, FLO Papers.

5. “Riverside Park,” *Chicago Tribune,* May 9, 1869.
6. Ibid.
7. Vaux to Olmsted, October 3, 1869, FLO Papers.

Buffalo Parks and Parkway System

1. A full account of Olmsted and Vaux’s work in Buffalo can be found in my book *The Best Planned City in the World: Olmsted, Vaux, and the Buffalo Park System* (Amherst, MA: Library of American Landscape History, 2013).

Frederic Edwin Church House / Olana, Hudson, NY

1. David Schuyler, *Sanctified Landscape: Writers, Artists, and the Hudson River Valley, 1820–1909* (Ithaca, NY: Cornell University Press, 2012), 6.
2. In *Country, Park & City: The Architecture and Life of Calvert Vaux* (New York: Oxford University Press, 1998), 206–15, I discuss my understanding of Vaux and Church’s relationship in the creation of the artist’s dream house.
3. Frederic Church to Mr. West, October 25, 1891, Archives of American Art, Smithsonian Institution.
4. Frederic Church to William Osborn, July 22, 1871, Osborn and Dodge Family Papers, 1726–1983, Princeton University Library Archival Collections.
5. Jervis McEntee, diary entry, July 22, 1872, Jervis McEntee Diaries, Archives of American Art, Smithsonian Institution.
6. Karen Zukowsky, “A New Jerusalem,” in *Frederic Church’s Olana on the Hudson: Art, Landscape, Architecture,* ed. Julia B. Rosenbaum and Karen Zukowski (New York: Rizzoli Electa, 2018).
7. Allegra K. Davis, “A Fitting Monument,” in *Afterglow: Frederic Church and the Landscape of Memory,* ed. A. K. Davis (Munich: Hirmer Verlag, 2024), 50–51.
8. Adam Yarinsky, quoted in “Governor Hochul Press Release, October 25, 2024,” https://olana.org/fccenter/.

Parliament Building, Ottawa, Ontario

1. Calvert Vaux, *Official correspondence, etc, in reference to plan for the arrangement of public grounds in front of the Parliament Buildings at Ottawa executed in accordance with the design prepared by C. Vaux, architect, New York, 1873–1879* (New York: Privately printed, 1882), 13.
2. Ibid., 12.
3. J. J. Stewart, “Notes on Calvert Vaux’s 1873 Design for the Public Grounds of the Parliament Buildings in Ottawa,” *Bulletin of the Association for Preservation Technology* 8 (1976): 6.
4. Ibid.

Bryn Mawr College, Bryn Mawr, PA

1. "In Lower Merion: Nature and Art in the Neighborhood of Bryn Mawr," *Philadelphia Times,* May 13, 1888.
2. Ibid.
3. Andropogon Associates, "Bryn Mawr College Campus Heritage Preservation Initiative" (2004), *Reports and Plans,* 1, available at https://repository.brynmawr.edu/facilities_plans/1.
4. Board of Managers, minutes, March 14, 1884, Bryn Mawr College Archives.
5. For a discussion of the Vassar plan, see Yvonne Elet, *The Campus Green: The Olmsted Firm's Designs for Vassar College,* exh. cat. (Poughkeepsie, NY: Vassar College, 2022), 4.
6. Bryn Mawr College became the Olmsted firm's job number 01435. See *The Master List of Design Projects of the Olmsted Firm,* 2nd ed. (Washington, DC: National Association for Olmsted Parks, 2008), 129.
7. In 1979 the forty-nine-acre Bryn Mawr campus was listed in the National Register of Historic Places.

Grace Church, Manhattan

1. Calvert Vaux, "Church Grounds," *The Churchman* 55 (June 4, 1887): 641–42.
2. Samuel Parsons Jr., "Grace Church Lawn," *The Century* 2 (October 1882): 954.
3. Ibid.
4. Vaux, "Church Grounds," 641.
5. Ibid.
6. Ibid.
7. Ibid.; Parsons Jr., "Grace Church Lawn," 954.
8. Vaux, "Church Grounds," 641–42.

Small Parks, Manhattan

1. Rachel Iannacone, "Open Space for the Underclass: New York's Small Parks (1880–1915)," PhD diss., University of Pennsylvania, 2005, vii.
2. Calvert Vaux, "The Gardens and Parks of Paris," in Calvert Vaux and Samuel Parsons Jr., *Concerning Lawn Planting* (New York: Orange Judd, 1881), 16.
3. An unsigned planting plan for Canal Park is preserved in the New York City Department of Records and Information Services, Municipal Archives.
4. Samuel Parsons Jr., "The Evolution of a City Square," *Scribner's Magazine* 12 (July 1892): 110.
5. "Opening Jackson Park," *New-York Tribune,* August 27, 1888.
6. Vaux may also have been responsible, together with Parsons, for the design of Greeley Square Park (1891), where the city erected a bronze statue by Alexander Doyle of the famous newspaperman who mistakenly thought that Central Park preserved an untouched natural landscape.

7. "Corlears Hook Park," *Garden and Forest* 7 (October 24, 1894): 422. The author was likely Charles Sprague Sargent.
8. Ibid.

Downing Park, Newburgh, NY

1. J. K. T., "Andrew and Charles Downing," *Boston Evening Transcript,* January 31, 1885.
2. Charles Darwin, *On the Origin of Species* (London, 1859), 85.
3. J. K. T., "Andrew and Charles Downing."
4. The Downing Park Planning Committee, formed in the 1980s, galvanized reclamation of the park after a period of decline, and the Garden Club of Orange and Dutchess Counties launched a major initiative to restore the historic landscape guided by the master plan created by Heritage Landscapes LLC in 1990. Today, Andrew Jackson Downing Memorial Park (Charles's name is no longer associated with it) is managed by the City of Newburgh in partnership with the Downing Park Conservancy. In 2022 the city council designated the "Top of the Circle," the former site of the Observatory, as the site of the Newburgh Colored Burial Ground Memorial. I discuss the park at further length in "Frederick Law Olmsted, Calvert Vaux, and Newburgh's Downing Park," *Hudson River Valley Review* 41 (spring 2025): 67–77.

John H. Wisner House / The Clearing, Summit, NJ

1. Samuel Parsons Jr., "Small Country Places," *Scribner's Magazine* 11 (March 1892): 308.

Robert B. Suckley House / Wilderstein, Rhinecliff, NY

1. John W. Ritch, *The American Architect, Comprising Original Designs of Cheap Country and Village Residences* (New York: C. M. Saxton, 1848), Design no. 2.
2. A rubbing of the petroglyph, which shows a man holding a tomahawk and a peace pipe, made by Robert Bowne Suckley is held in the Dutchess County Historical Society Collection.
3. [Stephen C. Foster], *Summer Memories: Long Branch and Wilderstein* (New York: Carlton & Porter, 1855), 98.
4. Cynthia Owen Philip, *Wilderstein and the Suckleys* (Rhinebeck, NY: Wilderstein Preservation, 2001), 23.
5. Downing Vaux to Robert Suckley, June 4, 1890, Robert Bowne Suckley Collection, Wilderstein Historic Site, Rhinebeck, NY.
6. Ibid.

Niagara Reservation, Niagara Falls, NY

1. In *The Best Planned City in the World: Olmsted, Vaux, and the Buffalo Park System* (Amherst, MA:

Library of American Landscape History, 2013), I give a detailed account of the Niagara Reservation project, including the decades-long effort to secure political support for it.

2. Calvert Vaux, "A National Park at Niagara," Letters from the People, *New York Tribune,* October 5, 1878.
3. Calvert Vaux, "The Preservation of Niagara Falls," *New-York Tribune,* July 7, 1883.
4. "Niagara Falls To-Day," *New York Times,* August 11, 1887.
5. Olmsted to J. T. Gardiner, October 3, 1879, James Terry Gardiner Papers, Manuscripts and Special Collections, New York State Library, Albany.
6. "General Plan for the Improvement of the Niagara Reservation, Report of Messrs. Olmsted and Vaux," *Supplemental Report of the Commissioners of the State Reservation at Niagara* (Albany, 1887), 31.
7. Ibid., 21.
8. Frederick Law Olmsted, quoted in "Park Notes," *Park and Cemetery* 5 (March 1895): 105.
9. Olmsted and Vaux, *General Plan,* 31.

Acknowledgments

This book would not have been possible without the generous support of many individuals. I am deeply grateful to the experts and scholars who offered me invaluable advice that helped shape ideas presented in this book. In particular, I thank Charles E. Beveridge, Series Editor, *The Papers of Frederick Law Olmsted* and the leading authority on the life and work of Vaux's renowned collaborator; Mosette Broderick, Director of Urban Design and Architecture Studies, New York University; Kerry Dean Carso, Professor of Art History, SUNY New Paltz; Emily T. Cooperman, Senior Architectural Historian, Cultural Resources, PS&S; Yvonne Elet, Professor of the History of Art and Architecture, Vassar College; Harvey K. Flad, Professor Emeritus of Geography, Vassar College; Anette Freytag, Professor of the History and Theory of Landscape Architecture, Rutgers University; Arleyn Levee, landscape historian; Sara Cedar Miller, Historian Emerita, Central Park Conservancy, and longtime champion of Calvert Vaux's genius on view in Central Park; the late David Schuyler, Professor of Humanities and American Studies, Franklin and Marshall College; and Kyle Toth, Principal Investigator of Architectural History, Cultural Resources, PS&S.

My sincere gratitude goes as well to the dedicated archivists and curators who allowed me access to their collections and who generously contributed visual materials, historical and modern, that enhanced the content and brought the narrative to life. I wish to thank Cynthia Brenwall, Conservator, City of New York Municipal Archives, who so liberally bestowed her expert knowledge of that cherished collection; Michele Clark, Archivist, U.S. Department of the Interior, National Park

Service, Frederick Law Olmsted National Historic Site; Clare Flemming, Research Archivist, The Olana Partnership; Larissa Glasser, MSLIS, Arnold Arboretum Horticultural Library and Archives; Heather Gring, Rare Book Curator, Buffalo & Erie County Public Library; Dick Julian, Riverside Historical Commission; Althea Meer, Systems & Digital Librarian, The LuEsther T. Mertz Library, The New York Botanical Garden; Allison Mills, College Archivist, Special Collections, Bryn Mawr College; Paul Pasquarello; Amy Peck, Archivist/Historian, Prospect Park Alliance; Rebecca Pou, Associate Director of Institutional Archives and Collections, Central Park Conservancy; Joe Santacroce, former Town Historian, Newburgh, NY; Andrew J. Semo, Rare Book Clerk, Buffalo & Erie County Public Library; Kelli Smith, Research & Collections Technician, New York State Office of Parks, Recreation and Historic Preservation; Cynthia Van Ness, Director of Library and Archives, Buffalo History Museum; and Duane Watson, Curator of Collections, Wilderstein Historic Site, Rhinebeck, NY.

I would also like to express my appreciation to individuals who shared with me their knowledge of various Vaux landscapes, and those individuals who welcomed me to sites that form the substance of this book. The list of those willing to accommodate my work embraces James Amemascor, Research Specialist, New Jersey Historical Society; the late Robert Benedict, Superintendent of Hillside Cemetery, Middletown, NY; Brian Dold, former Director of Planning and Advocacy, Buffalo Olmsted Parks Conservancy; Melanie Hasbrook, Director of Advancement and Marketing, The Olana Partnership; Fenella Hecksher, Board of Directors, Downing Park Conservancy; JoEllen Hundeland, author of *Hillside Cemetery, Middletown, New York: Beyond the Graves,* who photographed Hillside specially for this book; Jackie Kondel, Executive Director, Reeves-Reed Arboretum; William Krattinger, Historic Preservation Project Director, New York State Office of Parks, Recreation and Historic Preservation; Jon Lawson, Chair, Board of Directors, Calvert Vaux Preservation Alliance; Kathryn McCullough, Board of Directors, Calvert Vaux Preservation Alliance; Mary McTamany, City Historian, Newburgh, NY; Ann Neal Petri, former President, Olmsted Network; Mark Prezorski, Senior Vice President and Landscape Curator, The Olana Partnership; Sean Sawyer, Washburn & Susan Oberwager President, The Olana Partnership; Gregory J. Sokaris, Executive Director, Wilderstein Historic Site; the late David Vaux; Margaret Vaux; Trina Vaux; Susan Wyman, Trustee, Hillside Cemetery, Middletown, NY; and Christian Zimmerman, Vice President of Capital and Landscape Management, Prospect Park Alliance.

Finally, I am grateful to the team of people who brought this project to life. My thanks go to Jonathan Lippincott for the book's beautiful design, to Mary Bellino for her superb index, and to Carol Betsch, Managing Editor of LALH, for her diligent efforts on behalf of this book. Carol's meticulous editing and thoughtful questions helped refine the text at many turns. Beyond that, her enthusiasm and determination in finding appropriate images, and her personal photographs, lifted the project high over the finish line. I also extend my sincere thanks to Robin Karson, Executive Director, for the confidence she has expressed in my work, as well as for the care and attention she has devoted to its fruition.

Calvert Vaux, Landscape Architect was made possible by the generous support of the following:

Gerry Charitable Trust/BNY Mellon

Nancy R. Turner Fund
The Olmsted Fund

Furthermore: a program of the J. M. Kaplan Fund
Mr. and Mrs. John K. Notz, Jr.

Lauren Belfer and Michael Marissen
Nancy G. Frederick
Cynthia Hewitt and Daniel Holloway
Michael and Evelyn Jefcoat, in honor of Francis R. Kowsky, FSAH
Thomas Lemann, Parkside Foundation
Barbara Robinson, The Widgeon Point Charitable Foundation
Margaret D. Sullivan, in honor of Robin Karson, Hon. ASLA

Ann Abadie
John Winthrop Aldrich, in honor of Francis R. Kowsky, FSAH
Jeff Allen, ASLA
Philip and Shelley Belling
Laura Louise Breyer
Charles D. Burnham, ASLA
David B. Coleman
George W. Curry, FASLA
Rolf Diamant and Nora Mitchell, Vermont Community Foundation
James C. Differding, ASLA
Terese D'Urso, in honor of John Furlong
Jeffrey J. Dyer
Elsbeth T. Falk
Elisabeth French
Lisa Gimmy, ASLA, LEED AP
Carol Grove
Shannon Hackett
David Phelps Hamar
Esley Hamilton
Morrison and Fenella Heckscher, in honor of Francis R. Kowsky, FSAH
John and Judith Herdeg
Marian Hill
Cheryl and Kevin Hurley, in memory of Ann D. Wilhite
Will Jolley
21st Century Park on the Outer Harbor, in honor of Francis R. Kowsky, FSAH
David Kamp, FASLA
Katherine Koch
Sidney I. Landau
Lucy Lawliss, ASLA
Richard Longstreth
Evelyn and Joseph McGee
Margaret Jean McKee
Kathleen and James Metz
Keith N. Morgan, FSAH
Mary Eugenia Myer
Darwina Neal, FASLA
Carl R. Nold
Dr. and Mrs. W. Scott Peterson, Connecticut Community Foundation
Anne Neal Petri
Margaret E. Richardson
Elizabeth Barlow Rogers, Hon. ASLA
Marcia D. Schoettle
David Schuyler
Karen Sebastian, ASLA
Natalie Shivers, AIA
R. Drew Sondles
Joseph Peter Spang
Walter and Nesta Spink
Judith Steckler
Frederick Steiner
Rober A. M. Stern, FAIA
Catherine M. Stone
Nancy B. Taylor
Sam Watters
David W. White
Mary and John Wight
Dana and Joe Woody
Lloyd Zuckerberg

Index

Page numbers in italics refer to illustrations.